NUTRIBULLET

Soup Recipe Book

Low Carb

Nutribullet Soup Recipes for

WEIGHT LOSS, DETOX, ANTI-AGING

& So MUCH MORE!

STEPHANIE SHAW

Disclaimer

The NutriBullet™ is a registered trademark of Homeland Housewares, LLC. Stephanie Shaw or her works herein are not affiliated with the owner of the trademark and is not an authorized distributor of the trademark owner's products or services.

This publication has not been prepared, approved or licensed by NutriBullet ™ or Homeland Housewares, LLC.

Table of Contents

Chapter 1: Why Are Homemade Soups Good for You?

When you make soup at home, you have control over the variety and quality of the ingredients you are using. You can tailor the contents of the soup to make either a quick, healthy, nutritious and substantial meal or a healthy snack without the additives that can be found in canned and packet soups.

Flavouring your soup with herbs, spices, salt and pepper will produce not only tasty soups but soups that are filled with health benefits. Herbs and spices are loaded with vitamins and minerals. When you are making your soup at home, you are able to adjust the amount and type of spice according to your personal preference. Even when using salt and pepper, you have a choice. Using freshly ground pepper is not only tastier but the health benefits are greater. Unrefined sea salt instead of refined table salt will be preferable because of the various minerals present in trace amounts working synergistically; it can help with high blood pressure, fatigue and thyroid problems that have been associated with eating refined salt.

Using good quality oils such as olive oil, macadamia nut oil, coconut oil, butter from grass fed cows or even organic ghee (clarified butter) to cook your soup will boost the health benefits of your homemade soup. Using the appropriate heat level is essential in order not to cause oxidative stress; the heat level when using different cooking oils, have been stated in the recipes.

Making your own bone broth would be an option. Proponents of bone broth claim that bone broth is good for a variety of health complaints and there are others who have questioned the health benefits. When making your homemade bone broth, just ensure that your source of bones is reputable. If you prefer, for convenience, using store bought organic bouillon or stock cubes would be fine.

Making homemade vegetable broth is easily done, by simmering carrots, onions, garlic, fresh parsley, celery and a teaspoon of whole peppercorns for a few hours. Strain the mixture so you're left with a clear broth and season with sea salt. Include organic bones and apple cider vinegar if you want bone broth and cook for 24 hours in a slow cooker.

With your Nutribullet RX or any other Nutribullet models, nutritious and healthy soups will be fast and easy to prepare. It is an excellent way to increase your vegetable intake as well as that of your family. It is also a good way of introducing new vegetables to your diet. As long as vegetables are included in your diet, whether they are cooked or raw, you will reap the benefit.

It is complicated to compare the benefits of cooked versus raw vegetables. Take broccoli for an example. Indole is formed when broccoli is cooked. Indole helps to destroy precancerous cells, reducing the risk of cancer. However, cooking broccoli will damage myrosinase, an enzyme, which breaks down glucosinates into the compound sulforaphane. Sulforaphane may reduce the risk of stomach cancers because it fights the bacteria, Helicobacter pylori. The best way to ensure that you get most out of your vegetables is probably to eat them raw as well as cooked.

However, vegetables such as broccoli, collard greens, spinach, bok choy and kale are preferable consumed cooked, not only to increase the nutritional benefits that these vegetables provide, but also to remove the goitrogens which have a negative impact on your thyroid especially if you do have hypothyroidism. While some experts in the field of nutrition encourage cooking these vegetables, others are of the opinion that if you are including foods that contain iodine, e.g. seaweed, milk and dairy products, eggs, white fish and nuts in your diet, the amount of goitrogens you are consuming from your vegetables will not be a problem. If you do have problems with your thyroid and are not taking medication for it, it would be advisable to avoid having too much of these vegetables in their raw state and be sure to include foods containing iodine in your diet.

Whilst cooking vegetables is beneficial and will increase certain nutrients, keep in mind that if they are cooked over high heat for too long, the nutrients will be lost. When you are making your soup at home, you have control over the temperature and the cooking time, which makes it easier to produce soup that is highly nutritious and also taste just the way you like.

For those on a weight loss program, studies have repeatedly shown that when soup is consumed before a meal, people tend to eat less at that meal. It is important to ensure that you are getting sufficient nutrients while you are on a weight loss programme. Replacing a meal daily with a vegetable based soup is a good way to ensure you are getting those vitamins and minerals essential for good health; besides the vitamins and minerals, vegetables are rich in phytonutrients and fibre. They contain protein and carbohydrate. You will therefore feel satiated eating a bowl of vegetable based soup that has been made with healthy oils.

I am sure that you are now more enthused to making your own soup, so let's get started.

Chapter 2: The Nutritional Benefits of Some of the Ingredients Used in the Recipes

Soups come with countless nutritional benefits required to maintain a healthy body in every way. Choosing good quality ingredients are therefore essential for good quality soups that will benefit your body.

In this chapter, you will learn of the health benefits of some of the ingredients that you will be using in the recipes. Everyday ingredients that you have used many a time but may not necessarily have known the benefits they have been bestowing on you.

Tomatoes contain a wide range of beneficial nutrients and antioxidants, such as vitamins A and C, lycopene, alpha-lipoic acid, folic acid, beta-carotene and lutein. Studies have shown having a diet rich in tomatoes may lower the risk of certain types of cancers; recent studies have suggested that the lycopene and other antioxidants in tomatoes may play a role in protecting bone health in postmenopausal women. Research has also shown consuming tomatoes reduce the risk of heart disease.

Onions contain sulphur compounds and flavonoids that help with reducing the risks of developing various cancers, improve the health of your skin, nails and hair. Human studies have shown that consuming onions daily can increase bone density; this is especially beneficial in postmenopausal women and also reduces the risk of hip fractures. Onions have been shown to have anti-inflammatory and anti-bacterial properties; they provide protection to the heart when they are included in a diet rich in vegetables and fruits.

Garlic contains protective compounds including allium, allicin, quercetin, allyl sulfides, selenium and a large group of various organosulfur compounds. 1-2 cloves of garlic daily can protect your cardiovascular system because of its anti-inflammatory properties. It has anti-bacterial and anti-viral properties, and it can reduce your risk of developing various cancers.

Pulses (beans, grams, and lentils) provide protein, complex carbohydrates and soluble fibre, as well as being a significant source of vitamins and minerals, such as iron, zinc, folate, and magnesium; the soluble fibre in the pulses will improve your cholesterol levels, which will in turn have a positive effect on several other cardiovascular disease risk factors, such as blood pressure and inflammation. Being high in soluble fibre, it has a low glycaemic index. Low glycaemic index foods slow the release of glucose into the blood thus stabilising blood glucose and insulin levels, which is beneficial especially for diabetics.

Carrots are rich in anti-oxidant flavonoids, beta-carotene, vitamin B-complex, vitamin A and various minerals in ample amounts. Vitamin A helps maintain good eye health. Potassium helps control blood pressure and heart rate. Studies have shown that the flavonoids in carrots may offer protection from cancers of the oral cavity, colon, skin and lung. A Dutch study demonstrated that participants who ate at least 50-75 grams of carrots daily greatly reduced risk of developing cardiovascular disease.

Kale is rich in anti-oxidants, flavonoids, ALA (a building block of omega 3), fibre and protein. The flavonoids in kale have recently been discovered to have both anti-oxidants and anti-inflammatory properties. Steaming kale before consuming has cholesterol-lowering benefits. Kale been shown to reduce the risk of cancers and support the body's detoxification.

Celery is a rich source of flavonoids like lutein, zeaxanthin and beta-carotene. These flavonoids have been demonstrated in studies to lower inflammation, lower the risk of heart disease and enhance the immune system. Its high fibre content lowers your risk of developing colon cancer as it moves the food through your bowels quickly. Steaming celery retains the nutrients more so than boiling or blanching.

Avocado is a good source of monounsaturated fat, which is heart healthy. It lowers your LDL level while leaving your HDL level intact. While it contains carotenoids in itself, when eaten with other foods, it increases the carotenoid absorption from those foods. It has a high protein content where fruits are concerned and it is fibre rich.

Broccoli is an excellent vegetable to add to your repertoire of vegetables. It is high in calcium, selenium, omega-3 fatty acids, carotenoids lutein, zeaxanthin, beta-carotene, vitamins A, E, K, C and the range of vitamin B, magnesium, manganese and zinc. This combination of components have proven time and time again to heal your body, prevent cell damage and prevent cancer because of the antioxidant, anti-inflammatory, and pro-detoxification properties. It is also a good source of dietary fibre and protein.

Chestnuts, unlike other nuts and seeds, are relatively low in calories and are a rich source of mono-unsaturated fats. They are high in complex carbohydrates, contain some protein, and are a good source of dietary fibre, which helps lower blood cholesterol. The fibre is both soluble and insoluble. Chestnuts are a rich source of minerals, vitamins and phyto-nutrients that immensely benefit health. They are rich in folates, iron, calcium, magnesium, manganese, phosphorus, potassium, zinc and rich in vitamin B-complex and are gluten free. Potassium helps counter hypertensive action of sodium and lowers heart rate and blood pressure. Magnesium and phosphorus are important components of bone metabolism.

Quinoa is high in heart healthy fats such as monounsaturated fat with a small amount of alpha-linoleic acid, which is a plant omega 3. It is among only a few plant foods that contain the complete protein with all the 9 essential amino acids. Quinoa contains a high amount of insoluble fibre. It has been shown in recent studies that insoluble and soluble fibres are important when it comes to the managing and controlling high blood pressure. Optimally controlled blood pressure is an important factor in maintaining good heart health.

Barley contains nutrients such as the B vitamins thiamine and niacin, together with selenium, copper, and magnesium, which are useful in lowering cholesterol, high blood pressure and other risk factors associated with heart disease. The fibre content stabilises the blood glucose levels, beneficial especially in the management of diabetes; this reduces cholesterol levels and prevent constipation.

Kukicha is the aged roasted twigs and stems of black and green tea. The caffeine content is low. Rich is flavonoids, polyphenols, vitamin C, A and B-complex, calcium, selenium and other minerals

Chapter 3: Making Soup with the Nutribullet and Nutribullet RX is Fast and Easy

I used to make soups and smoothies in my Magic Bullet Nutribullet blender. I would cook the soup in the pan and cool it down thoroughly before I blended it in my Magic Bullet Nutribullet blender. I would then transfer the blended soup back into my pan and reheat it gently till it was piping hot before eating, because I like my soups hot. I finally decided to buy a Nutribullet RX so as to save time. I do make my soups with uncooked vegetables in my Nutribullet RX at times, but I prefer the taste of the soup when the vegetables are cooked before blending.

The ultra-fast cyclonic action of the Nutribullet RX blender speeds up the time you spend making creamy, tasty and nutritious soups. The speed at which the vegetables are blended in the Nutribullet RX ensures that the cell walls of the vegetables are broken down, releasing the nutrients. If you are not keen on adding milk to your soups, the Nutribullet RX will deliver creamy tasting soups without milk.

Method Using the Nutribullet RX:

1. Remove the peel off ingredients that have thick skins like avocado.

2. Chop all the ingredients into small, even-sized chunks. This will speed up cooking time, which will reduce the loss of phytonutrients that are destroyed by heat.

3. Set the smashed and chopped garlic aside for 10 minutes before cooking to allow the conversion of allicin into allicin to take place. Allicin has been studied widely and been shown to provide the health benefits that we obtain from garlic.

4. Sautéing the garlic and onion with a splash of water or stock and cooking the vegetables before blending brings out the flavours of the vegetables making your soup taste a lot better. Vegetables when boiled or steamed will supply your body with more antioxidants.

5. Allow the unblended soup to cool down before blending.

6. Assemble the blade to the cup securely, but do not over tighten, before adding in the cooked vegetables up to the MAX mark that is on the blender cup. Pour

in the broth reaching up to about half an inch below the MAX mark. If the level of the liquid covers the vegetables, your blended soup will be bubbly, however, this will not affect the taste of the soup.

7. The amount of liquid of choice stated in the recipes will produce soup with a very thick consistency. Use more liquid should you prefer soups that have a watery consistency. You could either add the broth to the soup mid-way of the blending process or after blending.

8. Your Nutribullet RX can be operated on two modes:

   a) When blending on the first mode, which is just switching on the blender using the button on the side. The blended mixture does get warm but is not steaming hot. The blender does not switch off automatically on this mode.

   b) When blending on the second mode (I refer to it as the soup mode in the recipes), the blender will switch off automatically after about 7 minutes of blending and you will have hot steaming soup. You will have to depress the button that is lit green for a few seconds till the light turns red. This button is situated in the front of the blender

9. For a coarser textured soup, blend the soup on soup mode and stop after 3-4 minutes. Pour the soup back into the pan and heat gently till piping hot.

Method using the other Nutribullet models:

1. Steps **1)** to **5)** are the same.
2. Fill the tall cup to the MAX point; secure the blade assembly.
3. Blend the soup to the required texture.
4. Pour into a pan, add more broth if desired and heat to serve hot.

Note:

The blades of any model of Nutribullet are sharp, so handle them with care. Read and follow the manufacturer's instruction for your safety and to avoid voiding the manufacturer's warranty.

Chapter 4: Soup Recipes for a Healthy Heart

White Kidney Bean Soup

(Serves 2)

Ingredients

- 2 cups (475 ml) liquid of choice (stock, broth or bouillon)
- 1 tbsp dried white kidney beans
- 1/4 cup (35 g) rutabaga/swede (chopped into small pieces)
- 1/2 cup (50 g)celery stalk (chopped)
- 2 large cloves garlic (peeled, crushed and minced)
- 1/2 cup (80 g) onion (peeled and chopped into small pieces)
- 1/4 cup (8 g) watercress (chopped)
- Sea salt and pepper to taste (freshly ground)
- 1/2 a slice of thinly sliced bread (lightly toasted and cut into shapes)
- 1/4 cucumber (thinly sliced for garnishing)

Instructions

1. Soak the kidney beans overnight, discard the water the next day and boil in fresh water till tender. Drain and set aside.
2. Heat the olive oil in a pan over low heat.
3. Add the garlic and onion with a splash of stock/broth and cook till the onion is translucent.
4. Add the broth, beans, celery and rutabaga/swede and bring to a gentle boil.
5. Lower the heat and simmer for 7-10 minutes. Allow to cool thoroughly.

Using the Nutribullet RX:

a) Pour the soup into the assembled Nutribullet RX cup and blade and blend it on soup mode.

b) Stir in the chopped watercress.

c) Transfer the soup into your serving bowl and season with freshly ground sea salt and pepper.

d) Garnish with the cucumber slices and a piece of the shaped toasted bread and serve.

Using other Nutribullet models:

a) Pour the soup into the Nutribullet cup and blend to the desired texture.

b) Transfer the blended soup back into the pan and heat gently till steaming hot.

c) Stir in the chopped watercress.

d) Transfer into your serving bowl and season with freshly ground sea salt and pepper.

e) Garnish with the cucumber slices and a piece of toasted shaped bread and serve.

Nutritional Information

- Calories - 125
- Carbohydrates - 17g - (6%)
- Protein - 8g - (16%)
- Total Fat - 3g - (5%)
- Fibre - 3g - (12%)

Percent Daily Values are based on a 2000 calorie diet.

Carrot Squash Thyme Soup

(Serves 2)

Ingredients

- 2 cups (475 ml) liquid of choice (stock, broth or bouillon)
- 1/2 cup (65 g) carrot (chopped into small pieces)
- 1/2 cup (70 g) acorn squash (peeled and chopped into small pieces)
- 1/2 cup (80 g) onion (peeled and chopped into small pieces)
- 3 large cloves garlic (peeled, crushed and minced)
- 2 tsp thyme leaves
- Sea salt and pepper to taste (freshly ground)
- 2 tbsp olive oil
- 1/4 cup (60 ml) yoghurt
- A handful of cilantro/coriander (chopped)

Instructions

1. Heat the olive oil in a pan over low heat.
2. Add the garlic and onion and a splash of broth cook till the onion is translucent.
3. Add the broth, thyme, chopped carrots and acorn squash and bring to a gentle boil.
4. Lower the heat and simmer till the vegetables are tender.
5. Allow the soup to cool thoroughly.

Using the Nutribullet RX:

a) Pour the soup into the assembled Nutribullet RX cup and blade and blend it on soup mode.

b) Transfer into your serving bowl and season with freshly ground sea salt and pepper.

c) Garnish with the chopped /coriander and a dollop of yoghurt and serve.

Using other Nutribullet models (may need to be blended in two batches):

a) Pour the soup into the Nutribullet cup and blend to the desired texture.

b) Transfer the blended soup back to the pan and heat gently till steaming hot.

c) Transfer into your serving bowl and season with freshly ground sea salt and pepper.

d) Garnish with the chopped cilantro/coriander and a dollop of yoghurt and serve.

Nutritional Information

- Calories - 238
- Carbohydrates - 19g - (6%)
- Protein - 7g - (14%)
- Total Fat - 15g - (23%)
- Cholesterol - 1mg - (0%)
- Fibre - 2g - (8%)

Percent Daily Values are based on a 2000 calorie diet.

Italian Tomato and Black Bean Soup

(Serves 2)

Ingredients

- 2 cups (475 ml) liquid of choice (stock, broth or bouillon)
- 1 tbsp dried black beans
- 1 cup (180 g) tomato (cut into small pieces)
- 1/2 cup (80 g) onion (peeled and chopped into small pieces)
- 3 cloves garlic (peeled, crushed and minced)
- 1/2 tsp oregano or Italian seasoning pepper
- 1 tbsp virgin olive oil
- Sea salt and pepper to taste (freshly ground)
- A handful of fresh chives (chopped)

Instructions

1. Soak the black beans overnight, discard the water the next day and boil in fresh water till tender. Drain and set aside.
2. Heat the olive oil in a pan over low heat.
3. Add the garlic and onion and a splash of the broth and cook till the onion is translucent.
4. Add the broth, chopped tomatoes, cooked kidney beans and oregano and bring to a gentle boil.
5. Lower the heat and simmer for 7-10 minutes.
6. Allow to cool thoroughly.

Using the Nutribullet RX:

a) Pour the soup into the assembled Nutribullet RX cup and blade and blend it on soup mode.

b) Transfer into your serving bowl and season with freshly ground sea salt and pepper.

c) Garnish with the chopped chives and serve.

d) Note: For a coarse texture, blend the soup for 3-5 minutes, transfer to a pan and heat gently to serve steaming hot soup.

Using other Nutribullet models (you may need to blend in two batches):

a) Pour the soup into the Nutribullet cup and blend to the desired texture.

b) Transfer the blended soup back to the pan and heat gently till steaming hot.

c) Transfer into your serving bowl and season with freshly ground sea salt and pepper.

d) Garnish with the chopped chives and serve.

Recipe Notes

For a coarse texture, blend the soup for 3-5 minutes, transfer to a pan and heat to serve piping hot soup.

Nutritional Information

- Calories - 153
- Carbohydrates - 13g - (4%)
- Protein - 7g - (14%)
- Total Fat - 8g - (12%)
- Fibre - 3g - (12%)

Percent Daily Values are based on a 2000 calorie diet.

Mixed Vegetable Soup

(Serves 2)

Ingredients

- 2 cups (475 ml) liquid of choice (stock or broth or bouillon)
- 1/2 cup (45 g) broccoli (diced)
- 1/4 cup (50 g) collard greens (chopped)
- 1/4 cup (25 g) celery stalk (chopped)
- 1/4 cup (45 g) tomato (cut into small pieces)
- 1/4 cup (40 g) onion (peeled and chopped into small pieces)
- 2 cloves garlic (peeled, crushed and minced)
- Sea salt and pepper to taste (freshly ground)
- 1 tbsp olive oil
- 2 tsp spring onions (chopped)
- A handful parsley (chopped)

Instructions

1. Heat the olive oil in a pan over low heat.
2. Add the garlic and onion and a splash of broth and cook till the onion is translucent.
3. Add the broth, broccoli, celery and tomatoes and bring to a gentle boil.
4. Lower the heat and simmer for 5-6 minutes.
5. Add in the collard greens and stir for 1 minute and turn the heat off.
6. Allow to cool thoroughly.

Using the Nutribullet RX:

a) Pour the soup into the assembled Nutribullet RX cup and blade and blend it on soup mode.

b) Transfer into your serving bowl and season with freshly ground sea salt and pepper.

c) Garnish with the chopped spring onions and parsley and serve.

Using other Nutribullet models (may need to be done in two batches):

a) Pour the soup into the Nutribullet cup and blend to the desired texture.

b) Transfer the blended soup back to the pan and heat gently till steaming hot.

c) Transfer into your serving bowl and season with freshly ground sea salt and pepper.

d) Garnish with the chopped spring onions and parsley and serve.

Nutritional Information

- Calories - 136
- Carbohydrates - 8g - (3%)
- Protein - 7g - (14%)
- Total Fat - 9g - (14%)
- Fibre - 2g - (8%)

Percent Daily Values are based on a 2000 calorie diet.

Black Tuscan Kale (Cavolo Nero) Soup

(Serves 2)

Ingredients

- 2 cups (475 ml) liquid of choice (stock, broth or bouillon)
- 1/2 cup (125 g) Tuscan kale/cavolo nero (chopped)
- 1/2 cup (75 g) red sweet pepper (chopped)
- 1/4 cup (25 g) celery stalk (chopped)
- 1 1/2 tbsp dried fava/broad beans (soaked overnight)
- 1/4 cup (40 g) onion (peeled and chopped)
- 2 cloves garlic (peeled, crushed and minced)
- Sea salt and pepper to taste (freshly ground)
- 1 tsp dried oregano
- 1/2 tsp cayenne pepper (optional)
- 1 tbsp olive oil

Instructions

1. Soak the fava/broad beans overnight, discard the water the next day and boil in fresh water till tender. Drain and set aside.
2. Heat the olive oil in a pan over low heat.
3. Add the garlic and onion and a splash of broth and cook till the onion is translucent.
4. Add the broth, red sweet pepper, celery, oregano and cooked fava/broad beans and bring to a gentle boil.
5. Lower the heat and simmer for 5-6 minutes.
6. Add in the Tuscan kale/cavolo nero and stir for 1 minutes, and turn the heat off.
7. Allow to cool thoroughly.

Using the Nutribullet RX:

a) Pour the soup into the assembled Nutribullet RX cup and blade and blend it on soup mode.

b) Transfer into your serving bowl, season with freshly ground sea salt and pepper and serve.

Using other Nutribullet models (may need to be done in two batches):

a) Pour the soup into the Nutribullet cup and blend to the desired texture.

b) Transfer the blended soup back to the pan and heat gently till steaming hot.

c) Transfer into your serving bowl, season with freshly ground sea salt and pepper and serve.

Nutritional Information

- Calories - 158
- Carbohydrates - 12g - (4%)
- Protein - 8g - (16%)
- Total Fat - 9g - (14%)
- Fibre - 4g - (16%)

Percent Daily Values are based on a 2000 calorie diet.

Romaine, Avocado and Broccoli Soup

(Serves 2)

Ingredients

- 2 cups (475 ml) liquid of choice (stock, broth or bouillon)
- 1/2 cup (25 g) romaine lettuce (chopped)
- 1/4 cup (35 g) avocado (discard the skin and stone, and chop into small pieces)
- 1/4 cup (25 g) broccoli (chopped)
- 1/4 cup (40 g) potato (washed, peeled and chopped into small pieces)
- 1/4 cup (40 g) onion (peeled and chopped into small pieces)
- 2 cloves garlic (peeled, crushed and minced)
- Sea salt and pepper to taste (freshly ground)
- 2 tsp Italian seasoning
- 1 tbsp olive oil
- 2 tbsp spring onion (chopped for garnishing)

Instructions

1. Heat the olive oil in a pan over low heat.
2. Add the garlic and onion with a splash of broth and cook till the onion is translucent.
3. Add the broth, broccoli, potato and Italian seasoning and bring to a gentle boil.
4. Lower the heat and simmer till the potato pieces are soft and turn off the heat.
5. Allow the soup to cool down thoroughly.

Using the Nutribullet RX:

a) Pour the soup into the assembled Nutribullet RX cup and blade.
b) Add the chopped avocado and blend on soup mode.

c) Transfer into your serving bowl and season with freshly ground sea salt and pepper.

d) Garnish with the chopped spring onions and serve.

Using other Nutribullet models (may need to be done in two batches):

a) Pour the soup into the Nutribullet cup (you may need to blend in two batches).

b) Add the chopped avocado and blend to the desired texture.

c) Transfer the blended soup back to the pan and heat gently till steaming hot.

d) Transfer into your serving bowl; grind pepper and salt over the soup.

e) Garnish with the chopped spring onions and serve.

Nutritional Information

- Calories - 174
- Carbohydrates - 12g - (4%)
- Protein - 7g - (14%)
- Total Fat - 12g - (18%)
- Fibre - 4g - (16%)

Percent Daily Values are based on a 2000 calorie diet.

Quinoa and Tomato Soup

(Serves 2)

Ingredients

- 2 cups (475 ml) liquid of choice (stock, broth or bouillon)
- 1/4 cup (40 g) quinoa (cooked)
- 1/4 cup (40 g) potato (washed, peeled and chopped into small pieces)
- 1 cup (180 g) tomato (chopped into small pieces)
- 1/4 cup (40 g) onion (peeled and chopped)
- 3 cloves garlic (peeled, crushed and minced)
- Sea salt and pepper to taste (freshly ground)
- 1 tbsp olive oil
- A handful fresh basil (chopped)
- 1 tsp chilli sauce (optional)

Instructions

1. Cook the quinoa by adding one part of quinoa to two parts liquid in a pan.

2. Bring to a boil, reduce the heat and simmer for about 15 minutes till all the liquid has been absorbed. Turn off the heat and set aside.

3. Heat the olive oil in a pan over low heat.

4. Add the garlic and onion with a splash of broth and cook till the onion is translucent.

5. Add the broth, tomatoes and potatoes and bring to a gentle boil.

6. Lower the heat and simmer till the potato pieces are tender, turn off the heat.

7. Allow the soup to cool down thoroughly.

Using the Nutribullet RX:

a) Pour the soup into the assembled Nutribullet RX cup and blade, and blend on soup mode.

b) Transfer into your serving bowl; mix in the fresh basil and cooked quinoa.

c) Grind pepper and salt over the soup and serve with the chilli sauce.

Using other Nutribullet models (may need to be done in two batches):

a) Pour the soup into the Nutribullet cup and blend to the desired texture.

b) Transfer the blended soup back to the pan and heat gently till steaming hot.

c) Transfer into your serving bowl and mix in the fresh basil and cooked quinoa.

d) Grind pepper and salt over the soup and serve with the chilli sauce.

Recipe Notes

Cook the quinoa by adding one part of quinoa to two parts liquid in a pan. Bring to a boil, reduce the heat and simmer for about 15 mins.

Nutritional Information

- Calories - 182
- Carbohydrates - 18g - (6%)
- Protein - 8g - (16%)
- Total Fat - 9g - (14%)
- Fibre - 3g - (12%)

Percent Daily Values are based on a 2000 calorie diet.

Mushroom, Barley and Cashew Nut Soup

(Serves 2)

Ingredients

- 2 cups (475 ml) liquid of choice (stock, broth or bouillon)
- 1 1/2 tbsp dried whole grain barley
- 1/4 cup (30 g) carrot (chopped)
- 1/2 cup (35 g) mushroom (coarsely chopped)
- 1/2 cup (50 g) celery stalk (chopped)
- 1/4 cup (40 g) onion (peeled and chopped into small pieces)
- 2 large cloves garlic (peeled, crushed and minced)
- 1 tsp dried thyme
- 1 tbsp olive oil
- Apple cider vinegar to taste (optional)
- Sea salt and pepper to taste (freshly ground)
- 2 tbsp lightly pan roasted cashew nuts (chopped coarsely for topping)

Instructions

1. Soaked the barley overnight, discard the water the next day and cook the barley in a new batch of water. Boil till tender.

2. Heat the olive oil in a pan over low heat.

3. Add the garlic and onion with a splash of broth and cook till the onion is translucent.

4. Add the broth, carrots, celery, mushrooms, cooked barley and thyme and bring to a gentle boil.

5. Lower the heat and simmer till the barley is tender, turn off the heat and allow to cool down thoroughly.

Using the Nutribullet RX:

a) Pour the soup into the assembled Nutribullet RX cup and blade and blend on soup mode.

b) Season with apple cider vinegar and freshly ground sea salt and pepper.

c) Transfer into your serving bowl, top the soup with cashew nuts and serve the soup hot.

Using other Nutribullet models (you may need to blend in two batches):

a) Pour the soup into the Nutribullet cup and blend to the desired texture.

b) Transfer the blended soup back to the pan and heat gently till steaming hot.

c) Season with apple cider vinegar and freshly ground sea salt and pepper.

d) Transfer into your serving bowl, top the soup with cashew nuts and serve the soup hot.

Nutritional Information

- Calories - 205
- Carbohydrates - 16g - (5%)
- Protein - 9g - (18%)
- Total Fat - 12g - (18%)
- Fibre - 3g - (12%)

Percent Daily Values are based on a 2000 calorie diet.

Brown Onion and Cheese Soup

(Serves 2)

Ingredients

- 2 cups (475 ml) liquid of choice (stock, broth or bouillon)
- 1/2 cup (80 g) onions (peeled and chopped into small pieces)
- 2 cloves garlic (peeled, crushed and minced)
- 1/4 cup (35 g) sweet potato (washed, peeled and cut into small pieces)
- 1/2 cup (110 g) quark or any soft low fat/low salt cheese of choice
- 2 tsp olive oil
- Sea salt and pepper to taste (freshly ground)
- 1/2 tsp mustard powder
- 2 tsp parsley (chopped)
- 1 tsp parsley (chopped for garnishing)

Instructions

1. Heat the olive oil in a pan over low heat.
2. Add the garlic and onion with a splash of broth and cook till the onion is translucent.
3. Add the broth and sweet potato and bring to a gentle boil.
4. Lower the heat and simmer till the potato pieces are tender and turn off the heat.
5. Allow to cool thoroughly.

Using the Nutribullet RX:

a) Pour the soup into the assembled Nutribullet RX cup and blade and blend on soup mode. Midway, remove the plastic cover and pour in the quark, with the mustard powder and the parsley.

b) Season with freshly ground sea salt and pepper.

c) Transfer into your serving bowl, garnish with the remaining chopped parsley and serve the soup hot.

Using other Nutribullet models (you may need to blend in two batches). :

a) Pour the soup into the Nutribullet cup and blend for 3 minutes.

b) Add in the quark, mustard powder and parsley and continue blending.

c) Transfer the blended soup back into the pan and heat gently till steaming hot.

d) Season the soup with freshly ground sea salt and pepper to taste.

e) Transfer into your serving bowl, garnish with remaining chopped parsley and serve the soup hot.

Nutritional Information

- Calories - 159
- Carbohydrates - 11g - (4%)
- Protein - 11g - (22%)
- Total Fat - 7g - (11%)
- Cholesterol - 3mg - (1%)
- Fibre - 1g - (4%)

Percent Daily Values are based on a 2000 calorie diet.

Asparagus and Navy Bean Soup

(Serves 2)

Ingredients

- 2 cups (475 ml) liquid of choice (stock, broth or bouillon)
- 1 cup (135 g) asparagus (chopped)
- 1 1/2 tbsp dried navy beans
- 1/4 cup (40 g) onion (peeled and chopped into small pieces)
- 2 cloves garlic (peeled, crushed and minced)
- 1 tbsp olive oil
- A handful fresh basil leaves
- Sea salt and pepper to taste (freshly ground)
- 1/2 cup (65 g) asparagus (chopped)

Instructions

1. Soak the navy beans overnight, discard the water the next day and boil in fresh water till tender.
2. Heat the olive oil in a pan over low heat.
3. Add the garlic and onion with a splash of broth and cook till the onion is translucent.
4. Add the broth, asparagus and cooked navy beans and bring to a gentle boil.
5. Lower the heat and simmer for 5-6 minutes.
6. Turn off the heat, and allow to cool thoroughly.

Using the Nutribullet RX:

a) Pour the soup into the assembled Nutribullet RX cup and blade. The blending will have to be done in two batches.

b) Add the fresh basil and blend on soup mode.

c) Dish out into a serving bowl; grind sea salt and pepper over the soup.

d) Garnish with remaining chopped asparagus and serve the soup hot.

Using other Nutribullet models (may need to be done in two batches):

a) Pour the soup into the Nutribullet cup.

b) Add the fresh basil leaves and blend to the desired texture.

c) Transfer the blended soup back to the pan and heat gently till steaming hot.

d) Dish out into a serving bowl and grind sea salt and pepper over the soup.

e) Garnish with remaining chopped asparagus and serve the soup hot.

Nutritional Information

- Calories - 139
- Carbohydrates - 10g - (3%)
- Protein - 8g - (16%)
- Total Fat - 8g - (12%)
- Fibre - 3g - (12%)

Percent Daily Values are based on a 2000 calorie diet.

Chapter 5: Soup recipes for Detoxification

Detoxification is the process of cleansing the toxins from your body so that you will maintain good health. Your liver detoxifies your body and by eating the right foods, you will help your liver do its job better and you will also be helping your liver to function at its optimum for longer.

As a general concept, there are some basic rules you need to follow if you are detoxing. They are: drinking lots of water, getting adequate sleep and doing lighter exercises.

Using organic ingredients in the following recipes will be more beneficial for detoxing.

Beet Soup

(Serves 2)

Ingredients

- 2 cups (475 ml) liquid of choice (stock, broth or bouillon)
- 1/2 cup (70 g) beetroot (washed thoroughly, finely chopped)
- 1/4 cup (30 g) carrot (finely diced)
- 1/4 cup (25 g) leek (finely sliced)
- 1/2 cup (80 g) onion (peeled and chopped into small pieces)
- 2 cloves garlic (peeled, crushed and minced)
- 1 tsp coconut oil
- Sea salt to taste (freshly ground)
- 1/4 cup (30 g) pumpkin seeds

Instructions

1. Heat the coconut oil in a pan over medium heat, add the garlic and onion with a splash of broth and cook till the onion is translucent.

2. Add the broth, beetroot, carrot and leek and bring to a gentle boil.

3. Lower the heat and simmer till the vegetables are cooked.

4. Allow to cool thoroughly.

Using the Nutribullet RX:

a) Pour the contents of the pan into the assembled Nutribullet RX cup and blade; and blend on soup mode.

b) Transfer into a serving bowl, grind sea salt and pepper over the soup.

c) Garnish with pumpkin seeds and serve the soup hot.

Using other Nutribullet models (may need to be done in two batches):

a) Pour the soup into the Nutribullet cup and blend to the desired texture.

b) Transfer the blended soup back to the pan and heat gently till steaming hot.

c) Dish out into a serving bowl and grind sea salt and pepper over the soup.

d) Garnish with pumpkin seeds and serve the soup hot.

Nutritional Information

- Calories - 134
- Carbohydrates - 9g - (3%)
- Protein - 8g - (16%)
- Total Fat - 8g - (12%)
- Fibre - 2g - (8%)

Percent Daily Values are based on a 2000 calorie diet.

Collard and Mustard Greens Spring Soup

(Serves 2)

Ingredients

- 2 cups (475 ml) liquid of choice (stock, broth or bouillon)
- 1/4 cup (35 g) rutabaga/swede (peeled and chopped)
- 1/2 cup (30 g) mustard greens (chopped)
- 1/2 cup (100 g) collard greens (chopped)
- 1/4 cup (40 g) onion (peeled and chopped into small pieces)
- 2 tsp coconut oil
- 1 tsp ginger (peeled and chopped)
- Soy sauce (low salt organic) to taste
- Sea salt and pepper to taste (freshly ground)

Instructions

1. Heat the coconut oil in a pan over medium heat.
2. Add the onion and ginger with a splash of broth and cook till the onion is translucent.
3. Add in the broth and rutabaga/swede and bring to a gentle boil.
4. Lower the heat and simmer till the rutabaga/swede is tender.
5. Add in the mustard greens and collard greens to the pan and cook for a further 2-3 minutes, turn off the heat.
6. Allow the contents in the pan to cool thoroughly.

Using the Nutribullet RX:

a) Pour the contents of the pan into the assembled Nutribullet RX cup and blade, and blend on soup mode. Season the soup with soy sauce, freshly ground sea salt and pepper.

b) Serve the soup hot.

Using other Nutribullet models (you may need to blend in two batches):

a) Pour the soup into the Nutribullet cup and blend to the desired texture.

b) Transfer the blended soup back to the pan and heat gently till steaming hot.

c) Dish out into a serving bowl; grind sea salt and pepper over the soup.

d) Garnish with pumpkin seeds and serve the soup hot.

Nutritional Information

- Calories - 114
- Carbohydrates - 7g - (2%)
- Protein - 6g - (12%)
- Total Fat - 6g - (9%)
- Fibre - 2g - (8%)

Percent Daily Values are based on a 2000 calorie diet.

Cucumber Mint Soup

(Serves 2)

Ingredients

- 1 cup (240 ml) spring water
- 1 cup (240 ml) plain yoghurt
- 1 1/2 cups (150 g) cucumber (peeled and chopped)
- A handful mint leaves (chopped)
- 1 tbsp fresh lemon juice
- Sea salt and pepper to taste (freshly ground)

Instructions

1. Place all the ingredients in the Nutribullet/assembled Nutribullet RX cup and blade and blend to the desired texture.
2. Stir in the fresh lemon juice and season with freshly ground pepper and sea salt.
3. Chill the soup in refrigerator for 2 hours before eating it.

Nutritional Information

- Calories - 83
- Carbohydrates - 10g - (3%)
- Protein - 7g - (14%)
- Total Fat - 2g - (3%)
- Cholesterol - 8mg - (3%)
- Fibre - 0.5g - (2%)

Percent Daily Values are based on a 2000 calorie diet.

Spicy and Tender Green Vegetable Soup

(Serves 2)

Ingredients

- 1 cup (240 ml) liquid of choice (stock, broth or bouillon)
- 1 cup (240 ml) coconut cream or coconut milk
- 1/4 cup (25 g) celery stalk (chopped)
- 1/2 cup (15 g) spinach (chopped)
- 1/2 cup (75 g) green pepper (chopped into small pieces)
- 1/4 cup (40 g) onion (peeled and chopped into small pieces)
- 2 cloves garlic (peeled, crushed and minced)
- 1/2 tsp ground cumin
- 1/2 tsp ground ginger
- 1 tsp mint (dried)
- Sea salt and pepper to taste (freshly ground)

Instructions

1. Heat the coconut oil in a pan over medium to high heat.
2. Add the onion, cumin, garlic and ginger with a splash of water and cook till the onion is translucent.
3. Add the rest of the liquid, sweet pepper and celery and bring to a gentle boil.
4. Lower the heat and simmer for 5-6 minutes, stir in the spinach and turn off the heat.
5. Allow the contents in the pan to cool thoroughly.

Using the Nutribullet RX:

a) Pour the contents of the pan and coconut milk into the assembled Nutribullet RX cup and blade; and blend on soup mode. The blending will have to be done in two batches.

b) Season the soup with freshly ground sea salt and pepper; serve the soup hot.

Using other Nutribullet models (you may need to blend in two batches):

a) Pour the soup into the Nutribullet cup, add in the coconut milk and blend to the desired texture.

b) Transfer the blended soup back to the pan and heat gently till steaming hot.

c) Dish out into a serving bowl, grind sea salt and pepper over the soup and serve.

Nutritional Information

- Calories - 256
- Carbohydrates - 9g - (3%)
- Protein - 5g - (10%)
- Total Fat - 23g - (35%)
- Fibre - 2g - (8%)

Percent Daily Values are based on a 2000 calorie diet.

Leek and Zucchini (Courgette) Soup

(Serves 2)

Ingredients

- 2 cups (475 ml) liquid of choice (stock, broth or bouillon)
- 1/2 cup (45 g) leek (finely sliced)
- 1/2 cup (60 g) zucchini/courgette (chopped into small pieces)
- 1/4 cup (40 g) potato (washed, peeled and chopped into small pieces)
- 1/4 cup (40 g) onion (peeled and chopped into small pieces)
- 2 cloves garlic (peeled, crushed and minced)
- 1 tbsp coconut oil
- Sea salt and pepper to taste (freshly ground)

Instructions

1. Heat the coconut oil in a pan over medium to high heat.
2. Add the onion and garlic with a splash of broth, and cook till the onion is translucent.
3. Add the broth, leek, zucchini/courgette and potato and bring to a gentle boil.
4. Lower the heat and simmer till the potato is cooked.
5. Allow the contents in the pan to cool thoroughly.

Using the Nutribullet RX:

a) Pour the contents of the pan into the assembled Nutribullet RX cup and blade, and blend on soup mode. Season the soup with freshly ground sea salt and pepper and serve the soup hot.

Using other Nutribullet models (you may need to blend in two batches):

a) Pour the soup into the Nutribullet cup and blend to the desired texture.

b) Transfer the blended soup back to the pan and heat gently till steaming hot.

c) Dish out into a serving bowl, grind sea salt and pepper over the soup and serve.

Nutritional Information

- Calories - 148
- Carbohydrates - 12g - (4%)
- Protein - 6g - (12%)
- Total Fat - 9g - (14%)
- Fibre - 1g - (4%)

Percent Daily Values are based on a 2000 calorie diet.

Avocado and Vegetable Soup

(Serves 2)

Ingredients

- 2 cups (475 ml) liquid of choice (stock, broth or bouillon)
- 1/4 cup (30 g) zucchini/courgette (chopped into small pieces)
- 1/4 cup (15 g) kale leaves (chopped)
- 1/4 cup (20 g) fresh green beans
- 1/4 cup (25 g) celery stalk (chopped)
- 1/2 cup (75 g) avocado (peeled and chopped)
- 3 cloves garlic (peeled, crushed and minced)
- 1 tbsp coconut oil
- Sea salt and pepper to taste (freshly ground)
- 1/2 cup (75 g) avocado slices
- A handful fresh parsley (chopped, for garnishing)

Instructions

1. Heat the coconut oil in a pan over medium to high heat.
2. Add the garlic with a splash of broth and cook for 1/2 minute.
3. Add the broth, zucchini/courgette, carrots, green beans and celery; bring to a gentle boil.
4. Lower the heat and simmer till the green beans are tender.
5. Stir in the kale and turn off the heat.
6. Allow the contents in the pan to cool thoroughly.

Using the Nutribullet RX:

a) Pour the contents of the pan and chopped avocado into the assembled Nutribullet RX cup and blade and blend on soup mode.

b) Season the soup with freshly ground sea salt and pepper.

c) Pour into a serving bowl and garnish with the avocado slices and chopped parsley and serve the soup hot.

Using other Nutribullet models (may need to blend in two batches):

a) Pour the soup into the Nutribullet cup, add in the chopped avocado and blend to the desired texture.

b) Transfer the blended soup back to the pan and heat gently till steaming hot.

c) Dish out into a serving bowl, grind sea salt and pepper over the soup, garnish with the avocado slices and chopped parsley and serve the soup hot.

Nutritional Information

- Calories - 236
- Carbohydrates - 12g - (4%)
- Protein - 8g - (16%)
- Total Fat - 19g - (29%)
- Fibre - 6g - (24%)

Percent Daily Values are based on a 2000 calorie diet.

Pea and Broccoli Soup with Herbs

(Serves 2)

Ingredients

- 2 cups (475 ml) liquid of choice (stock, broth or bouillon)
- 1/2 cup (65 g) garden peas (shelled fresh or frozen)
- 1/2 cup (45 g) broccoli (chopped into small pieces)
- 1/4 cup (40 g) onion (peeled and chopped into small pieces)
- 1 1/2 tbsp dried brown or green lentils
- 3 cloves garlic (peeled, crushed and minced)
- 1 tbsp olive oil
- 1 tbsp fresh thyme leaves
- Sea salt and pepper to taste (freshly ground)

Instructions

1. Soak the lentils overnight, discard the water the next day and cook the lentils in fresh water till tender.
2. Heat the olive oil in a pan over low heat, add the garlic and shallot with a splash of broth and cook till the shallot is translucent.
3. Add the broth, peas, broccoli, lentils and thyme; bring to a gentle boil.
4. Lower the heat and simmer for 7-10 minutes.
5. Allow the contents in the pan to cool thoroughly.

Using the Nutribullet RX:

a) Pour the contents of the pan into the assembled Nutribullet RX cup and blade and blend on soup mode. Season the soup with freshly ground sea salt and pepper.

b) Pour into a serving bowl and serve the soup hot.

Using other Nutribullet models (may need to blend in two batches):

a) Pour the soup into the Nutribullet cup and blend to the desired texture.

b) Transfer the blended soup back to the pan and heat gently till steaming hot.

c) Dish out into a serving bowl and season the soup with freshly ground sea salt and pepper and serve the soup hot.

Nutritional Information

- Calories - 185
- Carbohydrates - 18g - (6%)
- Protein - 10g - (20%)
- Total Fat - 9g - (14%)
- Fibre - 4g - (16%)

Percent Daily Values are based on a 2000 calorie diet.

Pumpkin Soup

(Serves 2)

Ingredients

- 2 cups (475 ml) liquid of choice (stock, broth or bouillon)
- 1 cup (115 g) pumpkin (diced into small pieces)
- 1/2 cup (80 g) onion (peeled and chopped into small pieces)
- 2 cloves garlic (peeled, crushed and minced)
- 1 tbsp olive oil
- 1 sprig fresh rosemary
- Sea salt and pepper to taste (freshly ground)

Instructions

1. Heat the olive oil in a pan over low heat, add the garlic and onion with a splash of broth and cook till the onion is translucent.
2. Add the broth, pumpkin and rosemary; bring to a gentle boil.
3. Lower the heat and simmer for 10-15 minutes. Allow the contents in the pan to cool thoroughly.

Using the Nutribullet RX:

a) Pour the contents of the pan into the assembled Nutribullet RX cup and blade and blend on soup mode.

b) Season the soup with freshly ground pepper and sea salt.

c) Dish out into a serving bowl and serve the soup hot.

Using other Nutribullet models (may need to blend in two batches):

a) Pour the soup into the Nutribullet cup and blend to the desired texture.

b) Transfer the blended soup back to the pan and heat gently till steaming hot.

c) Dish out into a serving bowl and season the soup with freshly ground sea salt and pepper and serve the soup hot.

Nutritional Information

- Calories - 139
- Carbohydrates - 11g - (4%)
- Protein - 6g - (12%)
- Total Fat - 8g - (12%)
- Fibre - 1g - (4%)

Percent Daily Values are based on a 2000 calorie diet.

Minty Sweet Pea with Ginger Soup

(Serves 2)

Ingredients

- 2 cups liquid of choice (stock, broth or bouillon)
- 1 cup (60 g) shelled fresh garden peas or frozen sweet peas
- 1/4 cup (25 g) celery stalk (chopped)
- 1/4 cup (40 g) shallot (diced finely)
- 1 tbsp fresh ginger (roughly chopped)
- 2 tbsp fresh mint leaves
- 1 tbsp olive oil
- Sea salt and pepper to taste (freshly ground)
- 1/2 cup (75 g) fresh peas
- Handful of mint leaves (for garnishing)

Instructions

1. Heat the olive oil in a pan over low heat, add the shallot and ginger with a splash of broth and cook till the shallot is translucent.
2. Add the broth and garden peas and bring to a gentle boil.
3. Lower the heat and simmer for 5 minutes.
4. Turn off the heat and allow the contents in the pan to cool thoroughly.

Using the Nutribullet RX:

a) Pour the contents of the pan and the mint into the assembled Nutribullet RX cup and blade, and blend on soup mode.

b) Season the soup with freshly ground pepper and sea salt.

c) Dish out into a serving bowl, garnish with the remaining peas and mint leaves and serve the soup hot.

Using other Nutribullet models (may need to blend in two batches):

a) Pour the soup into the Nutribullet cup, add the mint leaves and blend to the desired texture.

b) Transfer the blended soup back to the pan and heat gently till steaming hot.

c) Dish out into a serving bowl and season the soup with freshly ground sea salt and pepper.

d) Garnish with mint leaves and garden peas and serve the soup hot.

Nutritional Information

- Calories - 173
- Carbohydrates - 15g - (5%)
- Protein - 9g - (18%)
- Total Fat - 8g - (12%)
- Fibre - 4g - (16%)

Percent Daily Values are based on a 2000 calorie diet.

Broccoli and Arugula Soup

(Serves 2)

Ingredients

- 2 cups (475 ml) liquid of choice (stock, broth or bouillon)
- 1/2 cup (45 g) broccoli (chopped into small pieces)
- 1/2 cup (45 g) yellow onion (peeled and chopped into small pieces)
- 1/2 cup (10 g) arugula (rocket)
- 2 garlic clove (peeled, crushed and minced)
- 1 tbsp olive oil
- 1 tbsp fresh lemon juice
- Sea salt and pepper to taste (freshly ground)

Instructions

1. Heat the olive oil in a pan over low heat.
2. Add the garlic and onion with a splash of broth and cook till the onion is translucent.
3. Add the broth and broccoli and bring to a gentle boil.
4. Lower the heat and simmer till the broccoli is tender, stir in the arugula (rocket) and turn off the heat.
5. Allow the contents in the pan to cool thoroughly.

Using the Nutribullet RX:

a) Pour the contents of the pan into the assembled Nutribullet RX cup and blade and blend on soup mode.

b) Season the soup with freshly ground sea salt and pepper and lemon juice to taste.

c) Transfer into your serving bowl and serve the soup hot.

Using other Nutribullet models (may need to blend in two batches):

a) Pour the soup into the Nutribullet cup and blend to the desired texture.

b) Transfer the blended soup back to the pan and heat gently till steaming hot.

c) Dish out into a serving bowl and season the soup with freshly ground sea salt and pepper.

d) Garnish with mint leaves and garden peas and serve the soup hot.

Nutritional Information

- Calories - 141
- Carbohydrates - 6g - (2%)
- Protein - 6g - (12%)
- Total Fat - 11g - (17%)
- Fibre - 1g - (4%)

Percent Daily Values are based on a 2000 calorie diet.

Chapter 6: Soup Recipes for Weight Loss

Red Lentils, Carrot and Ginger Soup

(Serves 2)

Ingredients

- 2 cups (475 ml) liquid of choice (stock, broth or bouillon)
- 1/2 cup (65 g) carrot (peeled and diced finely)
- 1/2 cup (75 g) sweet pepper (chopped into small pieces)
- 1 1/2 tbsp dried red lentils
- 1/2 cup (80 g) onion (peeled and chopped into small pieces)
- 2 cloves garlic (peeled, crushed and minced)
- 2 tsp ginger (peeled and minced finely)
- 2 tsp organic coconut oil
- 1 tsp fresh thyme (minced)
- Sea salt and pepper to taste (freshly ground)
- 2 tbsp lightly roasted cashew nuts (coarsely chopped for garnishing)

Instructions

1. Soak the lentils overnight, discard the water the next day and cook the lentils in fresh water till tender.
2. Heat the coconut oil in a pan over medium heat, add the garlic, ginger and onion with a splash of broth and cook till the onion is translucent.
3. Add the broth, pepper, carrots, lentils and thyme and bring to a gentle boil.
4. Lower the heat and simmer till the carrot and lentils are cooked.
5. Allow the soup to cool thoroughly.

Using the Nutribullet RX:

a) Pour the contents of the pan into the assembled Nutribullet RX cup and blade and blend on soup mode.

b) Season the soup with freshly ground pepper and sea salt.

c) Pour out into a serving bowl and garnish with the lightly roasted cashew nuts and serve the soup hot.

Using other Nutribullet models (may need to be done in two batches):

a) Pour the soup into the Nutribullet cup and blend to the desired texture.

b) Transfer the blended soup back to the pan and heat gently till steaming hot.

c) Dish out into a serving bowl and season the soup with freshly ground sea salt and pepper.

d) Garnish with lightly roasted cashew nuts and serve the soup hot.

Nutritional Information

- Calories - 202
- Carbohydrates - 19g - (6%)
- Protein - 9g - (18%)
- Total Fat - 11g - (17%)
- Fibre - 4g - (16%)

Percent Daily Values are based on a 2000 calorie diet.

Sweet Potato and White Kidney Bean Soup

(Serves 2)

Ingredients

- 2 cups (475 ml) liquid of choice (stock, broth or bouillon)

- 1 1/2 tbsp dried cannellini beans

- 1 cup (135 g) sweet potato (washed, peeled and chopped into small pieces)

- 1/2 cup (80 g) onion (peeled and chopped into small pieces)

- 2 cloves garlic (peeled, crushed and minced)

- 2 tsp olive oil

- 1 tsp ground cumin

- 1/2 tsp smoked paprika

- Sea salt and pepper to taste (freshly ground)

Instructions

1. Soak the cannellini beans overnight, discard the water the next morning, and boil the beans in fresh water till tender. Set aside.

2. Heat the olive oil in a pan over low heat.

3. Sauté the garlic and onion with a splash of broth and cook till the onion is translucent.

4. Add the broth, sweet potato, cooked cannellini beans, cumin and paprika and bring to a gentle boil.

5. Lower the heat and simmer for 10-15 minutes.

6. Allow the contents of the pan to cool thoroughly.

Using the Nutribullet RX:

a) Pour the contents of the pan into the assembled Nutribullet RX cup and blade and blend on soup mode.

b) Season the soup with freshly ground pepper and sea salt and serve.

Using other Nutribullet models (may need to be blended in two batches):

a) Pour the soup into the Nutribullet cup and blend to the desired texture.

b) Transfer the blended soup back to the pan and heat gently till steaming hot.

c) Dish out into a serving bowl and season the soup with freshly ground sea salt and pepper, and serve the soup hot.

Nutritional Information

- Calories - 186
- Carbohydrates - 25g - (8%)
- Protein - 8g - (16%)
- Total Fat - 6g - (9%)
- Fibre - 4g - (16%)

Percent Daily Values are based on a 2000 calorie diet.

Summer Squash and Carrot Soup

(Serves 2)

Ingredients

- 2 cups (475 ml) liquid of choice (stock, broth or bouillon)
- 1/2 cup (55 g) yellow summer squash (chopped into small pieces)
- 1/2 cup (65 g) carrot (chopped into small pieces)
- 1/2 cup (80 g) red onion (peeled and chopped into small pieces)
- 2 garlic clove (peeled, crushed and minced)
- 1/2 tsp ground cumin
- 1/4 tsp ground cilantro/coriander
- 1 tbsp coconut oil
- Sea salt and pepper to taste (freshly ground)
- A handful fresh chives - sliced into 1/4" (0.5cm) lengths for garnishing

Instructions

1. Heat the coconut oil in a pan over medium heat; sauté the garlic, onion, cilantro/coriander and cumin with a splash of broth and cook till the onion is translucent.
2. Add the broth, summer squash and carrots and bring to a gentle boil.
3. Lower the heat and simmer till the carrots and squash are tender.
4. Turn off the heat and allow the contents of the pan to cool thoroughly.

Using the Nutribullet RX:

a) Pour the contents of the pan into the assembled Nutribullet RX cup and blade and blend on soup mode.

b) Season the soup with freshly ground pepper and sea salt, garnish with chives and serve.

Using other Nutribullet models (may need to be blended in two batches):

a) Pour the soup into the Nutribullet cup and blend to the desired texture.

b) Transfer the blended soup back to the pan and heat gently till steaming hot.

c) Dish out into a serving bowl and season the soup with freshly ground sea salt and pepper, garnish with chives and serve the soup hot.

Nutritional Information

- Calories - 139
- Carbohydrates - 11g - (4%)
- Protein - 6g - (12%)
- Total Fat - 9g - (14%)
- Fibre - 2g - (8%)

Percent Daily Values are based on a 2000 calorie diet.

Fresh Asparagus Garden Soup

(Serves 2)

Ingredients

- 1 cup (240 ml) liquid of choice (stock, broth or bouillon)
- 1 cup (240 ml) coconut milk
- 1/2 cup (65 g) asparagus (trimmed and cut into small pieces)
- 1/4 cup (40 g) red potato (washed, peeled and chopped into small pieces)
- 1/2 cup (80 g) onion (peeled and chopped into small pieces)
- 2 cloves garlic (peeled, crushed and minced)
- 1 tbsp coconut oil
- 1 tbsp lemon juice
- 1/4 tsp ground ginger
- 1/2 tsp curry powder
- Sea salt and pepper to taste (freshly ground)
- A handful fresh chives (finely chopped for garnishing)

Instructions

1. Heat the coconut oil in a pan over medium to high heat.
2. Add the garlic, onion, ginger and curry powder with a splash of broth and cook till the onion is translucent and aromatic.
3. Add the broth, potato and asparagus and bring to a gentle boil.
4. Lower the heat and simmer for 7-10 minutes. Allow the contents of the pan to cool thoroughly.

Using the Nutribullet RX:

a) Pour the contents of the pan and add in the coconut milk into the assembled Nutribullet RX cup and blade and blend on soup mode.

b) Season the soup with lemon juice, freshly ground pepper and sea salt and garnish with chives and serve.

Using other Nutribullet models (may need to be blended in two batches):

a) Pour the soup into the Nutribullet cup and blend to the desired texture.

b) Transfer the blended soup back to the pan; add the coconut milk and heat gently till steaming hot.

c) Dish out into a serving bowl and season the soup with lemon juice, freshly ground sea salt and pepper.

d) Garnish with chives and serve the soup hot.

Nutritional Information

- Calories - 325
- Carbohydrates - 16g - (5%)
- Protein - 4g - (8%)
- Total Fat - 29g - (45%)
- Fibre - 2g - (8%)

Percent Daily Values are based on a 2000 calorie diet.

Creamy Swiss Chard Soup with Rosemary Croutons

(Serves 2)

Ingredients

- 1 medium slice sourdough bread, cut into 1/2" (1 cm) cubes

- 2 tbsp virgin olive oil

- 1 garlic clove (peeled, crushed and minced)

- 1 tsp fresh rosemary (finely chopped)

- 2 cups (475 ml) liquid of choice (stock, broth or bouillon)

- 1 cup Swiss chard (chopped)

- 1/4 cup (20 g) eggplant (chopped)

- 1/4 cup (40 g) onion (peeled and chopped into small pieces)

- 2 cloves garlic (peeled, crushed and minced)

- 1 tbsp fresh rosemary (finely chopped)

- 1 tbsp butter

- Sea salt and pepper to taste (freshly ground)

- Freshly grated nutmeg for garnishing

Instructions

1. To prepare the croutons, set the oven to preheat at 375 °F (190 °C, Gas 5).

2. Toss bread cubes, garlic, olive oil, and rosemary in a large bowl until well combined.

3. Prepare a baking sheet and spread the bread cubes in a single layer. Set to bake for 12-15 minutes until crispy and golden.

4. In the meantime, prepare the soup.

5. Heat the butter in a pan over low to medium heat.

6. Sauté the onion, garlic, rosemary and a splash of broth and cook till the onion is translucent.

7. Add the remaining broth and potatoes and bring to a gentle boil.

8. Lower heat and simmer till the potato pieces are tender.

9. Stir in the Swiss chard and turn off the heat after 2-3 minutes.

10. Allow the contents of the pan to cool thoroughly.

Using the Nutribullet RX:

a) Transfer the soup into your assembled Nutribullet RX cup and blade and blend on soup mode.

b) Season the blended soup with nutmeg, freshly ground pepper and sea salt.

c) Garnish with the croutons and serve the soup hot.

Using other Nutribullet models (may need to be blended in two batches):

a) Pour the soup into the Nutribullet cup and blend to the desired texture.

b) Transfer the blended soup back to the pan and heat gently till steaming hot.

c) Dish out into a serving bowl and season with nutmeg, freshly ground sea salt and pepper.

d) Garnish with croutons and serve the soup hot.

Nutritional Information

- Calories - 281
- Carbohydrates - 16g - (5%)
- Protein - 7g - (14%)
- Total Fat - 21g - (32%)
- Cholesterol - 16mg - (5%)
- Fibre - 2g - (8%)

Percent Daily Values are based on a 2000 calorie diet.

Acorn Squash, Sweetcorn and Jalapeno Soup

(Serves 2)

Ingredients

- 2 cups (475 ml) liquid of choice (stock, broth or bouillon)
- 1/4 cup (35 g) acorn squash (peeled and cut into small pieces)
- 1/2 cup (80 g) fresh or frozen sweetcorn kernels
- 1/4 cup (40 g) red onion (peeled and chopped into small pieces)
- 1/2 jalapeno pepper (thinly chopped)
- 2 cloves garlic (peeled, crushed and minced)
- 1/2 tsp dried oregano
- Sea salt and pepper to taste (freshly ground)
- 1 tbsp butter
- 1 tbsp lime juice and zest
- 1 cup (140 g) cooked chicken (shredded)
- A handful of cilantro/coriander (finely chopped for garnishing)
- 1 roasted red pepper (thinly sliced for garnishing)

Instructions

1. Heat the butter in a saucepan over low to medium heat.
2. Add onion, garlic, oregano and a splash of broth and cook till the onion is translucent.
3. Add the broth, acorn squash, corn kernels and jalapeno pepper and bring to a gentle boil.
4. Lower heat and simmer till the acorn squash is cooked.
5. Allow the contents of pan to cool thoroughly.

Using the Nutribullet RX:

a) Transfer the soup into your assembled Nutribullet RX cup and blade and blend on soup mode.

b) Season with pepper and salt and stir in the lime juice and zest.

c) Garnish with the shredded chicken, cilantro/coriander and red pepper strips and serve the soup hot.

Using other Nutribullet models (may need to be blended in two batches):

a) Pour the soup into the Nutribullet cup and blend to the desired texture.

b) Transfer the blended soup back to the pan and heat gently till steaming hot, season with pepper and salt and stir in the lime juice and zest.

c) Dish out into a serving bowl, garnish with the shredded chicken, cilantro/coriander and red pepper strips and serve the soup hot.

Nutritional Information

- Calories - 289
- Carbohydrates - 19g - (6%)
- Protein - 25g - (50%)
- Total Fat - 13g - (20%)
- Cholesterol - 68mg - (23%)
- Fibre - 3g - (12%)

Percent Daily Values are based on a 2000 calorie diet.

Pumpkin Coconut Curry Soup

(Serves 2)

Ingredients

- 2 cups (475 ml) coconut milk
- 1 cup (115 g) pumpkin (peeled and chopped into small pieces)
- 1/4 cup (25 g) celery stalk (chopped)
- 1/4 cup (40 g) onion (peeled and chopped into small pieces)
- 2 cloves garlic (peeled, crushed and minced)
- 1 tbsp olive oil
- 1 tbsp curry powder
- 1/2 tsp ground cumin
- 1/2 tsp ground turmeric
- 1/2 tsp ground cilantro/coriander
- Sea salt and pepper to taste (freshly ground)
- 2 tbsp fresh lemon juice
- 1 tbsp fresh cilantro/coriander (chopped coarsely for garnishing)
- 1/2 cup (25 g) cashew nuts (toasted lightly and chopped coarsely)

Instructions

1. Heat the olive oil in a saucepan over low heat.

2. Add onion, garlic, cumin, curry powder, turmeric and cilantro/coriander with a splash of water and cook till the onion is translucent and aromatic.

3. Add the coconut milk, pumpkin and celery and bring to a gentle boil.

4. Lower heat and simmer till the pumpkin is tender.

5. Allow the contents of the pan to cool thoroughly.

Using the Nutribullet RX:

a) Transfer the soup into your assembled Nutribullet RX cup and blade and blend on soup mode.

b) Season the soup with pepper and salt and stir in the lemon juice.

c) Transfer to a serving bowl; garnish with toasted cashew nuts and chopped cilantro/coriander and serve immediately.

Using other Nutribullet models (you may need to blend in two batches):

a) Pour the soup into the Nutribullet cup and blend to the desired texture.

b) Transfer the blended soup back to the pan and heat gently till steaming hot, season with freshly ground pepper and salt and stir in the lemon juice.

c) Dish out into a serving bowl, garnish with toasted cashew nuts and chopped cilantro/coriander and serve immediately.

Nutritional Information

- Calories - 656
- Carbohydrates - 27g - (9%)
- Protein - 7g - (14%)
- Total Fat - 63g - (97%)
- Fibre - 3g - (12%)

Percent Daily Values are based on a 2000 calorie diet.

Green (Puy) Lentil and Tomato Soup

(Serves 2)

Ingredients

- 2 cups (475 ml) liquid of choice (stock, broth or bouillon)
- 1/4 cup (25 g) celery stalk (chopped)
- 1 cup (180 g) tomato (cut into small pieces)
- 1 1/2 tbsp dried green/puy lentils
- 1/4 cup (40 g) onion (peeled and chopped into small pieces)
- 2 cloves garlic (peeled, crushed and minced)
- 1/4 tsp ground cloves
- 2 tbsp dry red wine
- 1 tbsp coconut oil
- Sea salt and pepper to taste (freshly ground)
- 1/4 tsp balsamic vinegar, or red wine vinegar
- A handful fresh parsley (chopped finely for garnishing)

Instructions

1. Soak the lentils overnight, rinse the next day and cook in fresh water till tender. Drain and set aside.
2. Heat the coconut oil in a pan over medium to high heat.
3. Add onion, garlic, cloves and a splash of broth and cook till the onion is translucent.
4. Add the remaining broth, wine, tomatoes, celery and lentils and bring to a gentle boil.
5. Lower heat and simmer for 5-7 minutes then turn off the heat.
6. Allow the contents of the pan to cool thoroughly.

Using the Nutribullet RX:

a) Transfer the soup into your assembled Nutribullet RX cup and blade and blend on soup mode.

b) Season with freshly ground pepper and sea salt and vinegar.

c) Serve the soup hot.

Using other Nutribullet models (may need to be blended in two batches):

a) Pour the soup into the Nutribullet cup and blend to the desired texture.

b) Transfer the blended soup back to the pan and heat gently till steaming hot.

c) Season with freshly ground pepper and salt and vinegar.

d) Dish out into a serving bowl and serve.

Nutritional Information

- Calories - 171
- Carbohydrates - 14g - (5%)
- Protein - 8g - (16%)
- Total Fat - 9g - (14%)
- Fibre - 4g - (16%)

Percent Daily Values are based on a 2000 calorie diet.

2-Bean with Sweet Potato Soup

(Serves 2)

Ingredients

- 2 cups (475 ml) liquid of choice (stock, broth or bouillon)
- 1 cup (135 g) sweet potato (washed, peeled and chopped into small pieces)
- 1 1/2 tbsp dried black beans
- 1 1/2 tbsp dried navy beans
- 1/2 cup (80 g) onion (peeled and chopped into small pieces)
- 2 cloves garlic (peeled, crushed and minced)
- 1 tbsp olive oil
- 1/2 tsp ground cumin
- 1/2 tsp ground coriander
- Sea salt and pepper to taste (freshly ground)
- 1 tbsp fresh lime juice

Instructions

1. Soak the beans overnight, rinse the next day and cook in fresh water. Boil till the beans are tender, drain and set aside.

2. Heat oil in a pan over low heat. Sauté the onion, garlic, cilantro/coriander and cumin with a splash of broth till the onion is translucent.

3. Add in the broth, diced sweet potatoes and beans and bring to a gentle boil.

4. Turn the heat down and simmer for 10-15 minutes.

5. Turn off the heat and allow to cool thoroughly.

Using the Nutribullet RX:

a) Remove 1/4 of the beans and potato from the soup and set aside.

b) Add the remaining contents of the pan to your assembled Nutribullet RX cup and blade and blend for 5 minutes.

c) Return the soup to the pan and add the reserved potato and beans.

d) Heat thoroughly, season with freshly ground pepper and sea salt and add the lime juice.

e) Dish out into a serving bowl and serve hot.

Using other Nutribullet models (may need to be blended in two batches):

a) Remove 1/4 of the potato and beans from the soup and set aside.

b) Pour the rest of the cooled soup into the Nutribullet cup and blend to the desired texture.

c) Transfer the blended soup back to the pan, add in the reserved beans and potato and heat gently till steaming hot.

d) Season with freshly ground pepper and salt and lime juice.

e) Dish out into a serving bowl and serve hot.

Nutritional Information

- Calories - 205
- Carbohydrates - 26g - (9%)
- Protein - 8g - (16%)
- Total Fat - 8g - (12%)
- Fibre - 4g - (16%)

Percent Daily Values are based on a 2000 calorie diet.

Cheddar, Cannellini Bean and Broccoli Soup

(Serves 2)

Ingredients

- 2 cups (475 ml) liquid of choice (stock, broth or bouillon)
- 1 cup (90 g) broccoli (trimmed and chopped into small pieces)
- 2 tbsp dried cannellini beans
- 1/4 cup (40 g) onion (peeled and chopped into small pieces)
- 2 cloves garlic (peeled, crushed and minced)
- 1 tbsp olive oil
- Sea salt and pepper to taste (freshly ground)
- 1/2 cup (55 g) cheddar cheese (grated)

Instructions

1. Soak the beans overnight, rinse the next day and cook in fresh water. Boil till the beans are tender, drain and set aside.

2. Heat oil in a pan over low heat. Sauté the onion and garlic with a splash of broth till the onion is translucent.

3. Add in the broth, broccoli and beans and bring to a gentle boil.

4. Turn the heat down and simmer for 5-6 minutes.

5. Allow the contents of the pan to cool thoroughly.

Using the Nutribullet RX:

a) Add the contents of the pan to your assembled Nutribullet RX cup and blade and blend on soup mode.

b) Season with freshly ground salt and pepper.

c) Serve the soup hot, garnished with the grated cheddar cheese.

Using other Nutribullet models (may need to be blended in two batches):

a)   Pour the soup into the Nutribullet cup and blend to the desired texture.

b)   Transfer the blended soup back to the pan and heat gently till steaming hot.

c)   Season with freshly ground pepper and salt.

d)   Dish out into a serving bowl and serve hot, garnished with the grated cheddar cheese.

Nutritional Information

- Calories - 277
- Carbohydrates - 14g - (5%)
- Protein - 16g - (32%)
- Total Fat - 18g - (28%)
- Cholesterol - 30mg - (10%)
- Fibre - 3g - (12%)

Percent Daily Values are based on a 2000 calorie diet.

Chapter 7: Soup Recipes for Healthy Skin

Eggplant and Fava/Broad Bean Soup

(Serves 2)

Ingredients

- 2 cups (475 ml) liquid of choice (stock, broth or bouillon)
- 1 cup (80 g) eggplant (chopped)
- 1 1/2 tbsp dried fava/broad beans
- 1/4 cup (40 g) onion (peeled and chopped)
- 2 cloves garlic (peeled, crushed and minced)
- 1 tbsp curry powder
- 1 tbsp cilantro/coriander (chopped)
- 1 tsp cumin seeds
- 1 tbsp coconut oil
- Sea salt and pepper to taste (freshly ground)
- A handful parsley (chopped)

Instructions

1. Soak the beans overnight, rinse the next day and cook in fresh water. Boil till the beans are tender, drain and set aside.

2. Heat the coconut oil in a pan over medium to high heat.

3. Add the onion, garlic, curry powder and cumin seeds with a splash of broth and sauté till the onion is translucent.

4. Add in the remaining broth, eggplant, cilantro/coriander and beans and bring to a gentle boil.

5. Turn the heat down and simmer for 5-6 minutes.

6. Allow the contents of the pan to cool thoroughly.

Using the Nutribullet RX:

a) Add the contents of the pan to your assembled Nutribullet RX cup and blade and blend on soup mode.

b) Season with freshly ground salt and pepper.

c) Serve the soup hot, garnished with chopped parsley.

Using other Nutribullet models (may be blended in two batches):

a) Pour the soup into the Nutribullet cup and blend to the desired texture.

b) Transfer the blended soup back to the pan and heat gently till steaming hot.

c) Season with freshly ground pepper and salt.

d) Dish out into a serving bowl and serve hot, garnished with chopped parsley.

Nutritional Information

- Calories - 143
- Carbohydrates - 10g - (3%)
- Protein - 7g - (14%)
- Total Fat - 9g - (14%)
- Fibre - 4g - (16%)

Percent Daily Values are based on a 2000 calorie diet.

Spring Greens and Potato Soup

(Serves 2)

Ingredients

- 1 cup (240 ml) milk
- 1 cup (240 ml) liquid of choice (stock, broth or bouillon)
- 1 cup (65 g) spring green (chopped)
- 1/2 cup (80 g) onion (peeled and chopped into small pieces)
- 1/2 cup (80 g) potato (washed, peeled and chopped into small pieces)
- 2 tsp butter
- Sea salt and pepper to taste (freshly ground)
- 8 asparagus spears (for garnishing)

Instructions

1. Heat a little butter in a small pan over low to medium heat.
2. Sauté asparagus spears in it. Remove and set aside for garnishing.
3. To prepare the soup, heat remaining butter in a pan over low to medium heat.
4. Add the onions with a splash of broth and sauté till the onion is translucent.
5. Add the remaining broth and potato and bring to a gentle boil.
6. Lower the heat and simmer until the potato pieces are tender.
7. Stir in the spring greens and cook for about 2 minutes, then turn off heat.
8. Allow the contents of the pan to cool thoroughly.

Using the Nutribullet RX:

a) Add the soup and milk to your assembled Nutribullet RX cup and blade and blend on soup mode.

b) Season with freshly ground sea salt and pepper.

c) Transfer to a serving bowl, garnish with the sautéed asparagus spears and serve immediately.

Using other Nutribullet models (may be blended in two batches):

a) Pour the soup and the milk into the Nutribullet cup and blend to the desired texture.

b) Transfer the blended soup back to the pan and heat gently till steaming hot.

c) Season with freshly ground pepper and salt.

d) Dish out into a serving bowl, garnish with the sautéed asparagus and serve immediately.

Nutritional Information

- Calories - 210
- Carbohydrates - 22g - (7%)
- Protein - 9g - (18%)
- Total Fat - 10g - (15%)
- Cholesterol - 22mg - (7%)
- Fibre - 3g - (12%)

Percent Daily Values are based on a 2000 calorie diet.

Baby Corn and Spinach Blend

(Serves 2)

Ingredients

- 2 cups (475 ml) liquid of choice (stock, broth or bouillon)
- 1/2 cup (15 g) spinach (chopped)
- 1/4 cup (41 g) baby corn (chopped into small pieces)
- 1/4 cup (35 g) sweet potato (washed, peeled and chopped into small pieces)
- 1/4 cup (40 g) onion (peeled and chopped into small pieces)
- 2 cloves garlic (peeled, crushed and minced)
- 1 tbsp olive oil
- Sea salt and pepper to taste (freshly ground)

Instructions

1. Heat the oil in a pan over low heat. Add the onion and garlic with a splash of broth.
2. Sauté the onion and garlic till the onion is translucent.
3. Add in the remaining broth, potato and baby corn and bring to a gentle boil.
4. Turn the heat down and simmer till the vegetables are tender.
5. Stir in the spinach, turn off the heat and allow the contents of the pan to cool down thoroughly.

Using the Nutribullet RX:

a) Add the contents of the pan to your assembled Nutribullet RX cup and blade and blend on soup mode.

b) Season with freshly ground sea salt and pepper.

c) Transfer to a serving bowl and serve hot.

Using other Nutribullet models (may need to be blended in two batches):

a) Pour the soup and the milk into the Nutribullet cup and blend to the desired texture.

b) Transfer the blended soup back to the pan and heat gently till steaming hot.

c) Season with freshly ground sea salt and pepper.

d) Dish out into a serving bowl and serve hot.

Nutritional Information

- Calories - 143
- Carbohydrates - 12g - (4%)
- Protein - 6g - (12%)
- Total Fat - 8g - (12%)
- Fibre - 1g - (4%)

Percent Daily Values are based on a 2000 calorie diet.

Sugar Snap Pea and Cilantro/Coriander Soup

(Serves 2)

Ingredients

- 2 cups (475 ml) liquid of choice (stock, broth or bouillon)
- 1 cup (85 g) sugar snap peas
- 1/4 cup (40 g) onion (peeled and chopped into small pieces)
- 2 cloves garlic (peeled, crushed and minced)
- 1 tbsp fresh ginger (finely chopped)
- 2 tbsp cilantro/coriander (finely chopped)
- 1 green chilli (finely chopped)
- 1/4 cup (20 g) fresh coconut (grated)
- 1 tbsp butter
- Sea salt and pepper to taste (freshly ground)
- 1 tbsp mint leaves (chopped)

Instructions

1. Heat the butter in a pan over medium heat. Sauté the onion, garlic, chilli and ginger with a splash of broth, till the onion is translucent.

2. Add in the remaining broth, coconut, garden peas and cilantro/coriander, and bring to a gentle boil.

3. Turn the heat down and simmer for 5 minutes.

4. Turn off the heat and allow the contents of the pan to cool down thoroughly.

Using the Nutribullet RX:

a) Add the contents of the pan to your assembled Nutribullet RX cup and blade and blend on soup mode.

b) Season with freshly ground salt and pepper.

c) Garnish with the chopped mint leaves and serve.

Using other Nutribullet models (may be blended in two batches):

a) Pour the soup and the milk into the Nutribullet cup and blend to the desired texture.

b) Transfer the blended soup back to the pan and heat gently till steaming hot.

c) Season with freshly ground sea salt and pepper.

Nutritional Information

- Calories - 170
- Carbohydrates - 12g - (4%)
- Protein - 7g - (14%)
- Total Fat - 11g - (17%)
- Cholesterol - 16mg - (5%)
- Fibre - 3g - (12%)

Percent Daily Values are based on a 2000 calorie diet.

Lettuce Soup

(Serves 2)

Ingredients

- 2 cup (475 ml) liquid of choice (stock, broth or bouillon)
- 1 1/2 cups (70 g) romaine lettuce (chopped)
- 1/4 cup (40 g) onion (peeled and chopped into small pieces)
- 1/4 cup (40 g) potato (washed, peeled and chopped into small pieces)
- 1 tbsp butter
- Sea salt and pepper to taste (freshly ground)

Instructions

1. Heat the butter in a pan over low to medium heat. Sauté the onion with a splash of water until the onion is translucent.

2. Add in the broth and potato and bring to a gentle boil.

3. Turn the heat down and simmer for 5 minutes or till the potato pieces are tender.

4. Turn off the heat and add in the romaine lettuce.

5. Allow the contents of the pan to cool down thoroughly.

Using the Nutribullet RX:

a) Add the contents of the pan to your assembled Nutribullet RX cup and blade and blend on soup mode.

b) Season with freshly ground sea salt and pepper.

c) Serve the soup while it is still hot to enjoy the flavour.

Using other Nutribullet models (may need to be blended in two batches):

a) Pour the soup and the milk into the Nutribullet cup and blend to the desired texture.

b) Transfer the blended soup back to the pan and heat gently till steaming hot.

c) Season with freshly ground sea salt and pepper.

d) Dish out into a serving bowl and serve hot.

Nutritional Information

- Calories - 124
- Carbohydrates - 8g - (3%)
- Protein - 6g - (12%)
- Total Fat - 8g - (12%)
- Cholesterol - 16mg - (5%)
- Fibre - 1g - (4%)

Percent Daily Values are based on a 2000 calorie diet.

Butternut Squash with Sweet Carrots and Apple Soup

(Serves 2)

Ingredients

- 2 cups (475 ml) liquid of choice (stock or broth)
- 1/2 cup (70 g) butternut squash (chopped into small squares)
- 1/2 cup (60 g) green apple (chopped into small squares)
- 1/4 cup (65 g) carrot (chopped into small pieces)
- 1/4 cup (40 g) onion (peeled and chopped into small pieces)
- 2 cloves garlic (peeled, crushed and minced)
- 1 tbsp olive oil
- Sea salt and pepper to taste (freshly ground)
- 1 bay leaf
- 1 tsp ground nutmeg

Instructions

1. Heat the olive oil in a pan over low heat. Sauté the onion, garlic and nutmeg with a splash of broth until fragrant and the onion is translucent.

2. Add in the rest of the broth, butternut squash, carrot, apple and bay leaf and bring to a gentle boil.

3. Turn the heat down and simmer till the carrot and squash pieces are tender.

4. Turn off the heat and allow the contents of the pan to cool down thoroughly.

Using the Nutribullet RX:

a) Remove the bay leaf; pour the contents of the pan to your assembled Nutribullet RX cup and blade and blend on soup mode.

b) Season with freshly ground sea salt and pepper.

c) Pour out into a bowl and serve.

Using other Nutribullet models (may need to be blended in two batches):

a) Remove the bay leaf; pour the soup into the Nutribullet cup and blend to the desired texture.

b) Transfer the blended soup back to the pan and heat gently till steaming hot.

c) Season with freshly ground sea salt and pepper.

d) Dish out into a serving bowl and serve hot.

Nutritional Information

- Calories - 134
- Carbohydrates - 16g - (5%)
- Protein - 3g - (6%)
- Total Fat - 7g - (11%)
- Fibre - 3g - (12%)

Percent Daily Values are based on a 2000 calorie diet.

Creamy Tomato and Carrot Soup

(Serves 2)

Ingredients

- 2 cups (475 ml) liquid of choice (stock, broth or bouillon)
- 1/2 cup (90 g) tomato (diced small cubes)
- 1/4 cup (30 g) carrot (peeled and chopped into small pieces)
- 1/2 cup (125 g) silken tofu (drained and diced into small cubes)
- 1/4 cup (40 g) onion (peeled and chopped into small pieces)
- 2 cloves garlic (peeled, crushed and minced)
- 2 tbsp tomato paste
- 1 tbsp olive oil
- Sea salt and pepper to taste (freshly ground)

Instructions

1. Heat the olive oil in a pan over low heat. Sauté the onion and garlic with a splash of water until fragrant and the onion is tender.

2. Stir in the tomato paste and cook for another minute, stirring constantly.

3. Add the remaining broth, tomato, carrot and tofu and bring to a gentle boil.

4. Turn the turn the heat down and simmer on low heat till the carrot pieces are tender.

5. Turn off the heat and allow the contents of the pan to cool down thoroughly.

Using the Nutribullet RX:

a) Transfer the contents of the pan in your assembled Nutribullet RX cup and blade and blend on soup mode.

b) Season with freshly ground sea salt and pepper and serve hot.

Using other Nutribullet models (may need to be blended in two batches):

a) Pour the soup into the Nutribullet cup and blend to the desired texture.

b) Transfer the blended soup back to the pan and heat gently till steaming hot.

c) Season with freshly ground sea salt and pepper.

d) Dish out into a serving bowl and serve hot.

Nutritional Information

- Calories - 172
- Carbohydrates - 12g - (4%)
- Protein - 9g - (18%)
- Total Fat - 10g - (15%)
- Fibre - 2g - (8%)

Percent Daily Values are based on a 2000 calorie diet.

Hearty Lentil and Vegetable Soup

(Serves 2)

Ingredients

- 2 cups (475 ml) liquid of choice (stock, broth or bouillon)
- 1/4 cup (60 g) button mushroom (chopped into small pieces)
- 1/4 cup (7.5 g) spinach (chopped)
- 1/4 cup (30 g) carrot (finely diced)
- 1/4 cup (30 g) yellow summer squash (finely diced)
- 1/4 cup (30 g) sweet potato (washed, peeled and chopped into small pieces)
- 2 tbsp dried green/puy lentils
- 1/4 cup (40 g) onion (peeled and chopped into small pieces)
- 2 cloves garlic (peeled, crushed and minced)
- 1 tbsp olive oil
- Sea salt and pepper to taste (freshly ground)

Instructions

1. Soak the lentils overnight. Discard the water the next day and cook the lentils in fresh water till tender. Drain and set aside.

2. Heat the olive oil in a pan over low heat. Sauté the onion and garlic with a splash of broth until fragrant and the onion is tender.

3. Add the remaining broth, mushrooms, carrot, squash, sweet potato and lentils and bring to a gentle boil.

4. Turn the turn the heat down and simmer on low heat till the vegetables are tender.

5. Stir in the chopped spinach and turn off the heat.

6. Allow the contents of the pan to cool down thoroughly

Using the Nutribullet RX:

a) Transfer the soup in your assembled Nutribullet RX cup and blade and blend on soup mode.

b) Season with freshly ground sea salt and pepper and serve hot.

Using other Nutribullet models (you may need to blend in two batches):

a) Pour the soup into the Nutribullet cup and blend to the desired texture.

b) Transfer the blended soup back to the pan and heat gently till steaming hot.

c) Season with freshly ground sea salt and pepper.

d) Dish out into a serving bowl and serve hot.

Nutritional Information

- Calories - 186
- Carbohydrates - 18g - (6%)
- Protein - 10g - (20%)
- Total Fat - 8g - (12%)
- Fibre - 6g - (24%)

Percent Daily Values are based on a 2000 calorie diet.

Tomato Blend with Italian Herbs and Roasted Pepper Soup

(Serves 2)

Ingredients

- 2 cups (475 ml) liquid of choice
- 1 cup (180 g) plum tomato (diced into small cubes)
- 1/2 cup (75 g) red sweet pepper (chopped into small pieces)
- 1/2 cup (80 g) onion (peeled and chopped into small pieces)
- 2 cloves garlic (peeled, crushed and minced)
- 1/4 tsp dried thyme
- 1 bay leave
- 1/2 tbsp fresh basil leaves (chopped)
- 1/2 tbsp fresh rosemary (chopped)
- 1 tsp organic apple cider vinegar
- 2 tsp tomato puree
- 1 tbsp olive oil
- Sea salt and pepper to taste (freshly ground)

Instructions

1. Heat the olive oil in a pan over low heat. Sauté the onion and garlic with a splash of broth until fragrant and the onion is tender.

2. Add the rest of the broth, tomatoes, peppers, tomato puree, apple cider vinegar, thyme, rosemary and bay leaves and bring to a gentle boil.

3. Turn the heat down and simmer on low heat for 20 minutes to allow the different flavours from the herbs to be infused into the soup.

4. Turn off the heat and allow the contents of the pan to cool down thoroughly.

Using the Nutribullet RX:

a) Transfer the contents of the pan in your assembled Nutribullet RX cup and blade and blend on soup mode.

b) Season with freshly ground sea salt and pepper.

c) Pour into a serving bowl and garnish with the chopped basil leaves and serve hot.

Using other Nutribullet models (may need to be blended in two batches):

a) Pour the soup into the Nutribullet cup and blend to the desired texture.

b) Transfer the blended soup back to the pan and heat gently till steaming hot.

c) Season with freshly ground sea salt and pepper.

d) Dish out into a serving bowl and serve hot.

Nutritional Information

- Calories - 126
- Carbohydrates - 13g - (4%)
- Protein - 4g - (8%)
- Total Fat - 7g - (11%)
- Fibre - 3g - (12%)

Percent Daily Values are based on a 2000 calorie diet.

Roasted Carrot and Celery Soup

(Serves 2)

Ingredients

- 2 cups (475 ml) liquid of choice (stock or broth or bouillon)
- 1/2 cup (65 g) carrot (peeled and diced into small pieces)
- 1/2 cup (50 g) celery stalk (chopped)
- 1/2 cup (80 g) onion (peeled and chopped into small pieces)
- 2 cloves garlic (peeled, crushed and minced)
- 1 tbsp fresh ginger (grated)
- 1/2 tbsp butter
- Sea salt and pepper to taste (freshly ground)

Instructions

1. Heat the butter in a pan over medium heat. Sauté the onion, ginger and garlic with a splash of broth until fragrant and the onion is tender.

2. Add the rest of the broth, carrots and celery and bring to a gentle boil.

3. Turn the heat down and simmer on low heat till the vegetable pieces are tender.

4. Turn off the heat and allow the contents of the pan to cool down thoroughly.

Using the Nutribullet RX:

a) Transfer the soup in your assembled Nutribullet RX cup and blade and blend on soup mode.

b) Season with freshly ground sea salt and pepper.

c) Pour out into a serving bowl and serve hot.

Using other Nutribullet models (may need to be blended in two batches):

a) Pour the soup into the Nutribullet cup and blend to the desired texture.

b) Transfer the blended soup back to the pan and heat gently till steaming hot.

c) Season with freshly ground sea salt and pepper.

d) Dish out into a serving bowl and serve hot.

Nutritional Information

- Calories - 83
- Carbohydrates - 11g - (4%)
- Protein - 3g - (6%)
- Total Fat - 3g - (5%)
- Cholesterol - 8mg - (3%)
- Fibre - 2g - (8%)

Percent Daily Values are based on a 2000 calorie diet.

Chapter 8: Soup Recipes for Energy Boost

Minestrone Soup

(Serves 2)

Ingredients

- 2 cups (475 ml) liquid of choice (stock, broth or bouillon)
- 1/4 cup (30 g) carrot (chopped)
- 1/4 cup (25 g) celery stalk (chopped)
- 1/4 cup (40 g) potato (washed, peeled and chopped into small pieces)
- 1/4 cup (45 g) tomato (diced into small cubes)
- 1 tbsp (15 g) dried cannellini or butter beans
- 1/4 cup (15 g) Savoy cabbage (coarsely shredded)
- 1/4 cup (40 g) onion (peeled and finely diced)
- 2 cloves garlic (peeled, crushed and minced)
- 1 tbsp olive oil
- 2 tbsp tomato puree
- Sea salt and pepper to taste (freshly ground)
- A handful fresh basil leaves (chopped)

Instructions

1. Soak the beans overnight, discard the water the next day and boil the beans in fresh water till tender. Drain the beans and set aside.

2. Heat the butter in a pan over medium heat. Sauté the onion and garlic with a splash of broth until fragrant and the onion is tender.

3. Add the rest of the broth, carrot, potatoes, tomatoes, cabbage and celery and bring to a gentle boil.

4. Turn the heat down and simmer on low heat till the vegetable pieces are tender.

5. Turn off the heat and allow the contents of the pan to cool down thoroughly.

Using the Nutribullet RX:

a) Transfer the soup to your assembled Nutribullet RX cup and blade.

b) Add the beans and tomato puree and blend for 2-3 minutes to produce a coarsely textured soup.

c) Transfer the coarsely blended soup back to the pan and heat gently till steaming hot.

d) Season with freshly ground sea salt and pepper.

e) Dish out into a serving bowl, garnish with the basil leaves and serve hot.

Using other Nutribullet models (may need to be blended in two batches):

a) Pour the soup into the Nutribullet cup; add the beans and tomato puree and blend for 2-3 minutes to produce a coarsely textured soup.

b) Transfer the coarsely blended soup back to the pan and heat gently till steaming hot.

c) Season with freshly ground sea salt and pepper.

d) Dish out into a serving bowl, garnish with the basil leaves and serve hot.

Nutritional Information

- Calories - 158
- Carbohydrates - 14g - (5%)
- Protein - 7g - (14%)
- Total Fat - 9g - (14%)
- Fibre - 3g - (12%)

Percent Daily Values are based on a 2000 calorie diet.

Butternut Squash with Crème Fraîche and Chili Soup

(Serves 2)

Ingredients

- 2 cups (475 ml) liquid of choice (stock, broth or bouillon)
- 1 cup (140 g) butternut squash (peeled and chopped into small pieces)
- 1/2 cup (80 g) onion (peeled and chopped into small pieces)
- 2 cloves garlic (peeled, crushed and minced)
- 1 tsp fresh rosemary (finely chopped)
- 1 tbsp butter
- Sea salt to taste (freshly ground)
- 2 tbsp crème fraîche
- 1 red chilli (deseeded and chopped finely)

Instructions

1. Heat the butter in a pan over medium heat. Sauté the onion and garlic with a splash of broth until fragrant and the onion is tender.
2. Add the rest of the broth, butternut and rosemary and bring to a gentle boil.
3. Turn the heat down and simmer on low heat till the butternut squash pieces are tender.
4. Turn off the heat and allow the contents of the pan to cool thoroughly.

Using the Nutribullet RX:

a) Transfer the soup in your assembled Nutribullet RX cup and blade and blend on soup mode.

b) Season with freshly ground sea salt and pepper.

c) Pour out into a serving bowl and serve garnished with crème fraîche and the chopped red chilli.

Using other Nutribullet models (may be need to be blended in two batches):

a) Pour the soup into the Nutribullet cup; blend the soup to your desired texture.

b) Transfer the coarsely blended soup back to the pan and heat gently till steaming hot.

c) Season with freshly ground sea salt and pepper.

d) Dish out into a serving bowl and serve garnished with crème fraîche and the chopped red chilli.

Nutritional Information

- Calories - 214
- Carbohydrates - 16g - (5%)
- Protein - 8g - (16%)
- Total Fat - 14g - (22%)
- Cholesterol - 39mg - (13%)
- Fibre - 3g - (12%)

Percent Daily Values are based on a 2000 calorie diet.

Buttermilk-Avocado Soup with Seafood Salad

(Serves 2)

Ingredients

- 1 cup (240 ml) liquid of choice (stock or broth or bouillon)
- 1 cup (240 ml) buttermilk
- 1 cup (130 g) fresh tomatillos (chopped into small pieces)
- 1/2 cup (75 g) avocado (chopped)
- 1/4 cup (40 g) onion (peeled and finely diced)
- 1 tbsp butter
- 1 jalapeno pepper (seeded and finely chopped)
- 1/2 cup (75 g) red sweet pepper (washed, seeded and chopped finely)
- 1 tbsp fresh chives (chopped finely)
- 1 tsp fresh lemon juice
- 1 cup (225 g) crabmeat (cooked)
- 1/2 tsp orange zest (grated)

Instructions

1. In a mixing bowl, combine the crabmeat, sweet pepper, fresh chives, lemon juice and grated orange rind.
2. Toss till well combined and set aside.
3. Heat the butter in the pan over low to medium heat; sauté the garlic and onion with a splash of broth till the onion is translucent.
4. Add the broth and tomatillos and bring to a gentle boil; lower the heat and simmer for 5 minutes.
5. Turn off the heat and allow the contents of the pan to cool thoroughly.

Using the Nutribullet RX and other models of Nutribullet:

a) Transfer the contents to the assembled Nutribullet RX cup and blade or Nutribullet cup.

b) Add the buttermilk, avocado, and jalapeno pepper and blend for 5 minutes.

c) Transfer the soup content into a serving bowl.

d) Top with the crabmeat mixture and serve immediately.

Nutritional Information

- Calories - 332
- Carbohydrates - 23g - (8%)
- Protein - 25g - (50%)
- Total Fat - 15g - (23%)
- Cholesterol - 101mg - (34%)
- Fibre - 5g - (20%)

Percent Daily Values are based on a 2000 calorie diet.

Sweet Potato Soup

(Serves 2)

Ingredients

- 2 cups (475 ml) liquid of choice (stock, broth or bouillon)
- 1 cup (135 g) sweet potatoes (washed, peeled and chopped into small pieces)
- 1/2 cup (80 g) onion (peeled and chopped into small pieces)
- 2 cloves garlic (peeled, crushed and minced)
- 1 tbsp butter
- 1 thyme sprig
- Sea salt and pepper to taste (freshly ground)
- 1/4 cup (60 ml) Greek yoghurt
- 2 tbsp fresh dill (finely chopped)
- 1/4 cup (30 g) mature cheddar cheese (grated)
- 1/4 cup (25 g) spring onion (finely chopped)
- 1/2 cup (65 g) roasted chicken (shredded)

Instructions

1. Heat the butter in the pan over low to medium heat; sauté the garlic and onion till fragrant and the onion is translucent.
2. Add the broth, sweet potatoes, dill and thyme and bring to a gentle boil.
3. Lower the heat and simmer till the sweet potato pieces are tender.
4. Allow the contents of the pan to cool down thoroughly.

Using the Nutribullet RX:

a) Add the contents to the assembled Nutribullet RX cup and blade and blend on soup mode.

b) Season with freshly ground sea salt and pepper.

c) Pour the soup content into a serving bowl and mix in the yoghurt.

d) Garnish with the grated cheese, spring onion and shredded chicken and serve.

Using other Nutribullet models (may need to be blended in two batches):

a) Pour the soup into the Nutribullet cup; blend the soup to your desired texture.

b) Transfer the blended soup back to the pan and heat gently till steaming hot.

c) Season with freshly ground sea salt and pepper.

d) Dish out into a serving bowl and mix in the yoghurt.

e) Garnish with the grated cheese, spring onion and shredded chicken and serve.

Nutritional Information

- Calories - 314
- Carbohydrates - 23g - (8%)
- Protein - 22g - (44%)
- Total Fat - 15g - (23%)
- Cholesterol - 65mg - (22%)
- Fibre - 4g - (16%)

Percent Daily Values are based on a 2000 calorie diet.

Roasted Chestnut with Thyme Cream Soup

(Serves 2)

Ingredients

- 2 cups (475 ml) liquid of choice (stock, broth or bouillon)
- 1 cup (145 g) roasted chestnuts (roasted and chopped)
- 1/2 cup (80 g) onion (peeled and chopped into small pieces)
- 1/4 cup (30 g) carrot (chopped into small pieces)
- 2 cloves garlic (peeled, crushed and minced)
- 1 tbsp olive oil
- Sea salt and pepper to taste (freshly ground)
- 1 1/2 tsp fresh thyme leaves (finely chopped)
- 1/2 cup (120 ml) whipping cream

Instructions

1. Set the oven to preheat at 400 °F (200 °C, Gas 6).

2. Place the chestnuts in a roasting pan and roast for about 20 minutes or until done.

3. Peel and chop the chestnuts coarsely and set aside.

4. Heat the olive oil in the pan over low heat; sauté the garlic and onion till fragrant and the onion is translucent.

5. Add the broth, chestnuts, carrot and thyme and bring to a gentle boil.

6. Lower the heat and simmer till the carrot pieces are tender.

7. Allow the contents of the pan to cool.

Using the Nutribullet RX:

a) Add the contents to the assembled Nutribullet RX cup and blade and blend on soup mode.

b) Season with freshly ground sea salt and pepper.

c) Meanwhile, add some sea salt to the cream and whip until the cream forms soft peaks.

d) When the soup is done, transfer into a serving bowl.

e) Top with the whipped cream and serve.

Using other Nutribullet models (may be need to be blended in two batches):

a) Pour the soup into the Nutribullet cup; blend the soup to your desired texture.

b) Transfer the blended soup back to the pan and heat gently till steaming hot.

c) Season with freshly ground sea salt and pepper.

d) Meanwhile, add some sea salt to the cream and whip until the cream forms soft peaks.

e) Dish out the soup into a serving bowl, top with the whipped cream and serve.

Nutritional Information

- Calories - 404
- Carbohydrates - 46g - (15%)
- Protein - 8g - (16%)
- Total Fat - 21g - (32%)
- Cholesterol - 41mg - (14%)
- Fibre - 5g - (20%)

Percent Daily Values are based on a 2000 calorie diet.

Vichyssoise

(Serves 2)

Ingredients

- 1/2 cup (120 ml) liquid of choice (stock, broth or bouillon)
- 1 cup (240 ml) almond milk
- 1 cup (90 g) leek (sliced thinly)
- 1/4 cup (35 g) sweet potato (washed, peeled and chopped into small pieces)
- 1 tbsp fresh chives (minced)
- Sea salt and pepper to taste (freshly ground)

Instructions

1. Heat the olive oil over low heat in pan, add the sliced leek and cook until soft.
2. Add in the chicken broth along with the sweet potato pieces.
3. Bring the mixture to a gentle boil.
4. Turn the heat down and simmer on low heat, until the sweet potato pieces are tender.
5. Turn off heat and allow the contents of the pan to cool thoroughly.

Using the Nutribullet RX or other Nutribullet models:

a) Transfer to your assembled Nutribullet RX cup and blade or your Nutribullet cup and blend for 6-7 minutes.

b) Pour into a serving bowl; season soup with freshly ground sea salt and pepper and stir in the almond milk.

c) Sprinkle with minced chives and serve.

d) If you like the colder version of the soup, chill in the refrigerator before serving.

Nutritional Information

- Calories - 71
- Carbohydrates - 11g - (4%)
- Protein - 3g - (6%)
- Total Fat - 2g - (3%)
- Fibre - 2g - (8%)

Percent Daily Values are based on a 2000 calorie diet.

Spinach and Fennel Soup with Pepper

(Serves 2)

Ingredients

- 2 cups (475 ml) liquid of choice (stock, broth or bouillon)
- 1/2 cup (15 g) fresh spinach (chopped)
- 1/2 cup (35 g) fennel bulb (chopped into small pieces with the fronds removed)
- 1/4 cup (20 g) leek (finely sliced)
- 1/4 cup (40 g) shallots (finely chopped)
- 1 tbsp fresh thyme (finely chopped)
- 1 bay leaf
- 1 tbsp olive oil
- 1 tsp lemon zest (grated)
- 2 tsp fresh lemon juice
- 1/4 cup (60 ml) Greek yoghurt
- 1/2 cup (75 g) red sweet pepper
- Sea salt and pepper to taste (freshly ground)

Instructions

1. Drizzle the sweet pepper with olive oil and roast in the oven till tender.
2. Heat the olive oil in the pan over low heat; sauté the shallot till fragrant and translucent.
3. Add the broth, fennel, leek, bay leaf and thyme and bring to a gentle boil.
4. Lower the heat and simmer till the vegetables are tender.
5. Stir in the spinach and turn off the heat.
6. Allow the contents of the pan to cool thoroughly.

Using the Nutribullet RX:

a) Remove the bay leaf and add the contents to the assembled Nutribullet RX cup and blade and blend on soup mode.

b) Season with freshly ground sea salt and pepper.

c) In a separate Nutribullet cup, add the yoghurt, roasted sweet pepper, lemon rind and lemon juice and blend until smooth.

d) Pour the soup in a serving bowl and season with salt and pepper, and garnish with the yoghurt and sweet pepper puree.

e) Serve and enjoy the flavours.

Using other Nutribullet models (may need to be blended in two batches):

a) Remove the bay leaf and transfer the contents of the pan to your Nutribullet cup.

b) Blend to your desired texture.

c) Pour the soup back to the pan and heat gently till piping hot.

d) Season with freshly ground sea salt and pepper.

e) In a separate Nutribullet cup, add the yoghurt, roasted sweet pepper, lemon rind and lemon juice and blend until smooth.

f) Dish out the soup into a serving bowl and garnish with the yoghurt and sweet pepper puree.

g) Serve and enjoy the flavours.

Nutritional Information

- Calories - 166
- Carbohydrates - 13g - (4%)
- Protein - 7g - (14%)
- Total Fat - 10g - (15%)
- Cholesterol - 6mg - (2%)
- Fibre - 2g - (8%)

Percent Daily Values are based on a 2000 calorie diet.

Squash and Corn Chowder Soup

(Serves 2)

Ingredients

- 2 cups (475 ml) liquid of choice (stock, broth or bouillon)
- 1/2 cup (55 g) yellow squash (chopped into small pieces)
- 1/4 cup (25 g) celery stalk (chopped)
- 1/2 cup (80 g) frozen corn kernels (thawed)
- 1/4 cup (40 g) onion (peeled and chopped into small pieces)
- 2 cloves garlic (peeled, crushed and minced)
- 1 tsp fresh thyme (finely chopped)
- 1 tbsp olive oil
- Sea salt and pepper to taste (freshly ground)
- 1/4 cup (30 g) mature cheddar cheese (grated)
- 1 cup (90 g) tiger prawns (cooked, shelled and deveined)
- 1/4 cup (40 g) frozen corn kernels (thawed)

Instructions

1. Heat the olive oil in the pan over low heat; sauté the onion till fragrant and translucent.
2. Add the broth, celery, squash, corn and thyme and bring to a gentle boil.
3. Lower the heat and simmer till the vegetables are tender.
4. Turn off the heat and allow the contents of the pan to cool down thoroughly.

Using the Nutribullet RX:

a) Add the contents to the assembled Nutribullet RX cup and blade; blend on soup mode.
b) Season with freshly ground sea salt and pepper.

c) Transfer into a serving bowl and garnish with the remaining corn, grated cheese and prawns and serve.

Using other Nutribullet models (the blending may have to be done in two batches):

a) Pour the soup into the Nutribullet cup; blend the soup to your desired texture.

b) Transfer the blended soup back to the pan and heat gently till steaming hot.

c) Season with freshly ground sea salt and pepper.

d) Dish out the soup into a serving bowl; garnish with the remaining corn, grated cheese and prawns and serve.

Nutritional Information

- Calories - 273
- Carbohydrates - 19g - (6%)
- Protein - 20g - (40%)
- Total Fat - 14g - (22%)
- Cholesterol - 80mg - (27%)
- Fibre - 2g - (8%)

Percent Daily Values are based on a 2000 calorie diet.

Cream of Asparagus Soup

(Serves 2)

Ingredients

- 1 cup (240 ml) liquid of choice (stock, broth or bouillon)
- 1 cup (240 ml) milk
- 1 1/2 cups (200 g) asparagus (sliced thinly)
- 1/4 cup (40 g) potato (peeled and chopped into small pieces)
- 1 garlic clove (peeled, crushed and minced)
- 1 bay leaf
- 3/4 tsp fresh thyme
- 1 dash ground nutmeg
- 1 tbsp butter
- Sea salt to taste (freshly ground)
- 1/2 tsp lemon zest (grated)
- A handful parsley (chopped)

Instructions

1. Heat the butter in the pan over medium heat; sauté the garlic with a splash of broth till fragrant.
2. Add the remaining broth, asparagus, potato, bay leaf and thyme and bring to a gentle boil.
3. Lower the heat and simmer till the vegetables are tender.
4. Turn off the heat and allow the contents of the pan to cool thoroughly.

Using the Nutribullet RX:

a) Remove the bay leaf and add the contents from the pan, with the milk, lemon zest and nutmeg to the assembled Nutribullet RX cup and blade.

b) Blend on soup mode; season with freshly ground sea salt and pepper.

c) Pour into a serving bowl and serve hot.

Using other Nutribullet models (may need to be blended in two batches):

a) Pour the soup into the Nutribullet cup and blend the soup to your desired texture.

b) Transfer the blended soup back to the pan and heat gently till steaming hot.

c) Season with freshly ground sea salt and pepper.

d) Dish out the soup into a serving bowl and garnish with chopped parsley and serve.

Nutritional Information

- Calories - 186
- Carbohydrates - 15g - (5%)
- Protein - 9g - (18%)
- Total Fat - 11g - (17%)
- Cholesterol - 28mg - (9%)
- Fibre - 3g - (12%)

Percent Daily Values are based on a 2000 calorie diet.

Red Lentil, Leek, Tuscan Kale (Cavolo Nero) with Lemon and Cilantro/Coriander Soup

(Serves 2)

Ingredients

- 2 cups liquid of choice (stock, broth or bouillon)
- 2 tbsp dried red lentils
- 1/2 cup (35 g) Tuscan kale/cavolo nero (chopped)
- 1/4 cup (20 g) leek (chopped)
- 1/4 cup (20 g) eggplant (chopped)
- 1/4 cup (40 g) onion (peeled and chopped into small pieces)
- 1 garlic clove (peeled, crushed and minced)
- 1 tbsp olive oil
- A handful of cilantro/coriander (chopped for garnishing)
- 1/2 lemon (juice)
- Sea salt (freshly ground) to taste

Instructions

1. Soak the red lentils overnight. Discard the water the next day and boil in fresh water till cooked. Drain and set aside.
2. Heat the olive oil in a pan over low heat; sauté the onion and garlic with a splash of broth until the onion is transparent.
3. Add the remaining broth, leek, eggplant and red lentils to the pan and bring the mixture to a gentle boil.
4. Lower the heat and simmer until the vegetables are cooked and soft.
5. Stir in the Tuscan kale/cavolo nero and cook for another minute.
6. Turn off the heat and leave to cool down thoroughly.

Using the Nutribullet RX:

a) In the assembled Nutribullet RX cup and blade, pour in the soup and blend on soup mode.

b) Season with freshly ground sea salt and pepper.

c) Mix in the lemon juice.

d) Serve the soup hot, garnished with chopped cilantro/coriander.

Using other Nutribullet models (you will need to blend in two batches):

a) Pour the soup into the Nutribullet cup and blend the soup to your desired texture.

b) Transfer the blended soup back to the pan and heat gently till steaming hot.

c) Season with freshly ground sea salt and pepper.

d) Mix in the lemon juice.

e) Dish out the soup into a serving bowl.

f) Garnish with chopped cilantro/coriander

g) Serve hot and enjoy!

Nutritional Information

- Calories - 174
- Carbohydrates - 16g - (5%)
- Protein - 9g - (18%)
- Total Fat - 8g - (12%)
- Fibre - 4g - (16%)

Percent Daily Values are based on a 2000 calorie diet.

Chapter 9: Soup Recipes for Anti-Aging Effects

Yellow Split Peas, White Cabbage, Tomato Soup

(Serves 2)

Ingredients

- 1 cup (240 ml) liquid of choice (stock, broth or bouillon)
- 1 cup (240 ml) coconut milk
- 2 1/2 tbsp dried yellow split peas
- 1/2 cup (45 g) white cabbage (chopped)
- 1/2 cup (90 g) tomatoes (chopped)
- 1/4 cup (40 g) onion (peeled and chopped into small pieces)
- 2 cloves garlic (peeled, crushed and minced)
- 2 tbsp ginger (finely chopped)
- 1 tbsp curry powder
- 1 tbsp organic ghee
- 1/2 organic lemon (juice and zest)
- Sea salt and pepper to taste (freshly ground)
- A handful cilantro/coriander (finely chopped)

Instructions

1. Soak the yellow split peas overnight. Discard the water the next day and boil in fresh water till cooked. Drain and set aside.

2. Heat the ghee in a pan over medium to high heat.

3. Sauté the onion, garlic, ginger and curry powder with a splash of broth until fragrant.

4. Add the remaining broth, coconut milk, white cabbage, tomatoes and beans and bring to a gentle boil.

5. Cover and simmer for 15 minutes.

6. Turn off the heat and cool thoroughly.

Using the Nutribullet RX

a) Pour the contents of the pan into your assembled Nutribullet RX cup and blade.

b) Add in the lemon zest and juice and blend on soup mode.

c) Season with freshly ground sea salt and pepper.

d) Pour the soup into a serving bowl, garnish with cilantro/coriander and serve.

Using other Nutribullet models (you may need to blend in two batches).

a) Pour the soup into the Nutribullet cup; add the lemon zest and juice.

b) Blend the soup to your desired texture.

c) Transfer the blended soup back to the pan and heat gently till steaming hot.

d) Season with freshly ground sea salt and pepper.

e) Dish out the soup into a serving bowl.

f) Garnish with cilantro/coriander and serve.

Nutritional Information

- Calories - 361
- Carbohydrates - 23g - (8%)
- Protein - 7g - (14%)
- Total Fat - 30g - (46%)
- Cholesterol - 18mg - (6%)
- Fibre - 6g - (24%)

Percent Daily Values are based on a 2000 calorie diet.

Fennel, Sweet Potato and Orange Soup

(Serves 2)

Ingredients

- 2 cups (475 ml) liquid of choice (stock, broth or bouillon)
- 3/4 cup (85 g) fennel (chopped)
- 1/2 cup (65 g) sweet potato (peeled and chopped into small pieces)
- 1/4 cup (40 g) shallot (peeled and finely chopped)
- 2 cloves garlic (peeled, crushed and minced)
- Sea salt and pepper to taste (freshly ground)
- 1 tbsp olive oil
- 2 tbsp fresh orange juice
- 1 tbsp of orange zest
- A handful fresh parsley (chopped)

Instructions

1. Heat the olive oil in a pan over low heat.
2. Sauté the shallot and onion with a splash of broth.
3. Cook until the onion is translucent.
4. Add the remaining broth, sweet potato and fennel and bring to a gentle boil.
5. Lower the heat and simmer till the potato is soft.
6. Turn off the heat and let the contents of the pan cool down thoroughly.

Using the Nutribullet RX:

a) Pour the contents of the pan into your assembled Nutribullet RX cup and blade; add the orange zest and juice.

b) Blend on soup mode; season with freshly ground sea salt and pepper.

c) Pour the soup into a serving bowl; garnish with parsley and serve

Using other Nutribullet models (may need to be blended in two batches):

a) Pour the soup into the Nutribullet cup; add the orange zest and juice.

b) Blend the soup to your desired texture.

c) Transfer the blended soup back to the pan and heat gently till steaming hot.

d) Season with freshly ground sea salt and pepper.

e) Dish out the soup into a serving bowl.

f) Garnish with parsley and serve.

Nutritional Information

- Calories - 169
- Carbohydrates - 18g - (6%)
- Protein - 7g - (14%)
- Total Fat - 8g - (12%)
- Fibre - 2g - (8%)

Percent Daily Values are based on a 2000 calorie diet.

Button Mushroom, Celery and Pumpkin Soup

(Serves 2)

Ingredients

- 2 cups (475 ml) liquid of choice (stock, broth or bouillon)
- 1/2 cup (120 g) button mushroom (chopped)
- 1/2 cup (50 g) celery stalk (chopped)
- 1/4 cup (30 g) pumpkin (peeled and chopped)
- 1/4 cup (40 g) onion (peeled and finely chopped)
- 2 cloves garlic (peeled, crushed and minced)
- Sea salt and pepper to taste (freshly ground)
- 1 tsp ground ginger
- 1 tsp ground cumin
- 1 tbsp olive oil
- A handful of thyme and rosemary (chopped)

Instructions

1. Heat the olive oil in a pan over low heat.

2. Sauté the garlic, onion, ginger and cumin with a splash of broth until the onion is translucent.

3. Add the remaining broth, mushroom, celery and pumpkin and bring to a gentle boil.

4. Lower the heat and simmer till the pumpkin is soft.

5. Turn off the heat and let the contents of the pan cool down thoroughly.

Using the Nutribullet RX:

a) Pour the contents of the pan into your assembled Nutribullet RX cup and blade.

b) Blend on soup mode; season with freshly ground sea salt and pepper.

c) Pour the soup into a serving bowl, garnish with thyme and rosemary and serve.

Using other Nutribullet models (you may need to blend in two batches):

a) Pour the soup into the Nutribullet cup.

b) Blend the soup to your desired texture Transfer the blended soup back to the pan and heat gently till steaming hot.

c) Season with freshly ground sea salt and pepper.

d) Dish out the soup into a serving bowl.

e) Garnish with thyme and rosemary and serve.

Nutritional Information

- Calories - 144
- Carbohydrates - 9g - (3%)
- Protein - 7g - (14%)
- Total Fat - 9g - (14%)
- Fibre - 3g - (12%)

Percent Daily Values are based on a 2000 calorie diet.

Onion and Apple Soup

(Serves 2)

Ingredients

- 2 cups (475 ml) liquid of choice (stock, broth or bouillon)
- 3/4 cup (65 g) yellow onion (peeled and chopped into small pieces)
- 1/2 cup (60 g) organic green apples (chopped into small pieces)
- 1/4 cup (20 g) leek (finely sliced)
- 1 tsp fresh thyme (finely chopped)
- 1 tbsp olive oil
- 1 tbsp juice and zest from an organic lemon

Instructions

1. Heat the olive oil in a pan over low heat.

2. Add onion, leek, and thyme with a splash of broth and sauté until fragrant and the leek and onion are translucent.

3. Add the remaining broth and green apples and bring the mixture to a gentle boil.

4. Turn down the heat and simmer for 5 minutes.

5. Turn off the heat and cool down thoroughly.

Using the Nutribullet RX:

a) Pour the contents of the pan into your assembled Nutribullet RX cup and blade.

b) Add in the lemon juice and zest and blend on soup mode.

c) Season with freshly ground sea salt and pepper.

d) Pour the soup into a serving bowl and serve.

Using other Nutribullet models:

a) Pour the soup into the Nutribullet cup; blend the soup to your desired texture (you may need to blend in two batches).

b) Transfer the blended soup back to the pan and heat gently till steaming hot.

c) Season with freshly ground sea salt and pepper. Stir in the orange juice and zest.

d) Dish out the soup into a serving bowl and serve.

Nutritional Information

- Calories - 166
- Carbohydrates - 10g - (3%)
- Protein - 6g - (12%)
- Total Fat - 12g - (18%)
- Fibre - 2g - (8%)

Percent Daily Values are based on a 2000 calorie diet.

Broccoli Leaves with Tomatoes and Rutabaga (Swede) Soup

(Serves 2)

Ingredients

- 2 cups (475 ml) liquid of choice (stock, broth or bouillon)
- 3/4 cup (70 g) broccoli leaves (chopped)
- 1/4 cup (35 g) rutabaga/swede (peeled and chopped into small pieces)
- 1/4 cup (45 g) tomatoes (chopped into small pieces)
- 1/4 cup (40 g) onion (peeled and thinly sliced)
- 2 cloves garlic (peeled, crushed and minced)
- 1 tbsp olive oil
- 1/2 tsp organic raw apple cider vinegar
- Sea salt and pepper to taste (freshly ground)
- A handful fresh basil (chopped)

Instructions

1. Heat the olive oil in a pan over low heat.
2. Add the onion and garlic with a splash of broth and sauté until fragrant.
3. Add the remaining broth, rutabaga/swede and tomatoes and bring the mixture to a gentle boil.
4. Turn down the heat and simmer till the rutabaga/ is soft.
5. Stir in the chopped broccoli leaves and turn off the heat after 2 minutes; allow to cool down thoroughly.

Using the Nutribullet RX:

a) Pour the contents of the pan into your assembled Nutribullet RX cup and blade.

b) Add in the apple cider vinegar and blend on soup mode.

c) Season with freshly ground sea salt and pepper.

d) Pour the soup into a serving bowl: garnish with chopped basil and serve.

Using other Nutribullet models (you may need to blend in two batches):

a) Pour the soup into the Nutribullet cup; blend the soup to your desired texture.

b) Transfer the blended soup back to the pan and heat gently till steaming hot.

c) Season with the apple cider vinegar, freshly ground sea salt and pepper.

d) Dish out the soup into a serving bowl, garnish with chopped basil and serve.

Nutritional Information

- Calories - 133
- Carbohydrates - 9g - (3%)
- Protein - 7g - (14%)
- Total Fat - 8g - (12%)
- Fibre - 2g - (8%)

Percent Daily Values are based on a 2000 calorie diet.

Sprouts, Cauliflower and Kale Soup

(Serves 2)

Ingredients

- 2 cups (475 ml) liquid of choice (stock, broth or bouillon)
- 1/2 cup (45 g) Brussels sprouts (chopped)
- 1/4 cup (25 g) cauliflower (chopped)
- 1/4 cup (15 g) kale (chopped)
- 1/4 cup (30 g) carrot (chopped into small pieces)
- 1/4 cup (40 g) onion (peeled and chopped into small pieces)
- 2 cloves garlic (peeled, crushed and minced)
- 1 tbsp olive oil
- Sea salt and pepper to taste (freshly ground)
- 1 tsp ginger (peeled and finely chopped)
- 1/2 tsp turmeric

Instructions

1. Heat the olive oil in the pan over low heat; sauté the ginger, garlic and onion with a splash of broth until fragrant and the onion is translucent.
2. Add the broth, brussel sprouts, cauliflower, carrot and turmeric and bring to a gentle boil.
3. Lower the heat and simmer till the vegetables are tender.
4. Turn off the heat and cool the contents of the pan thoroughly.

Using the Nutribullet RX:

a) Add the contents to the assembled Nutribullet RX cup and blade; blend on soup mode.

b) Season with freshly ground sea salt and pepper.

c) Pour into a serving bowl and serve.

Using other Nutribullet models (you may need to blend in two batches):

a) Pour the soup into the Nutribullet cup; blend the soup to your desired texture.

b) Transfer the blended soup back to the pan and heat gently till steaming hot.

c) Season with freshly ground sea salt and pepper.

d) Dish out the soup into a serving bowl and serve.

Nutritional Information

- Calories - 136
- Carbohydrates - 9g - (3%)
- Protein - 7g - (14%)
- Total Fat - 8g - (12%)
- Fibre - 2g - (8%)

Percent Daily Values are based on a 2000 calorie diet.

Nourishing Nettle Soup

(Serves 2)

Ingredients

- 2 cups (475 ml) liquid of choice (stock, broth or bouillon)
- 1 cup (30 g) young nettle leaves (wear gloves and wash)
- 1/4 cup (7.5 g) fresh spinach (chopped)
- 1/4 cup (35 g) sweet potato (washed, peeled and chopped into small pieces)
- 1/4 cup (40 g) onion (peeled and finely chopped)
- 3 cloves garlic (peeled, crushed and minced)
- 1 tbsp olive oil
- A dash of ground nutmeg
- Sea salt and white pepper (freshly ground) to taste
- 2 tbsp plain yoghurt

Instructions

1. Heat the olive oil in a pan over low heat.
2. Add the onion and garlic with a splash of broth and sauté until fragrant.
3. Add the remaining broth, sweet potato and nutmeg and bring to a gentle boil.
4. Turn down the heat and simmer till the sweet potato is tender.
5. Stir in the nettle leaves and spinach and turn off the heat after 2 minutes.
6. Allow the contents of the pan to cool down thoroughly.

Using the Nutribullet RX:

a) Pour the contents of the pan into your assembled Nutribullet RX cup and blade and blend on soup mode.

b) Season with freshly ground sea salt and pepper.

c) Pour the soup into a serving bowl, drizzle the yoghurt over the soup and serve.

Using other Nutribullet models (you may need to blend in two batches):

a) Pour the soup into the Nutribullet cup and blend the soup to your desired texture.

b) Transfer the blended soup back to the pan and heat gently till steaming hot.

c) Season with freshly ground sea salt and pepper.

d) Dish out the soup into a serving bowl, drizzle the yoghurt over the soup and serve.

Nutritional Information

- Calories - 141
- Carbohydrates - 10g - (3%)
- Protein - 7g - (14%)
- Total Fat - 9g - (14%)
- Cholesterol - 1mg - (0%)
- Fibre - 1g - (4%)

Percent Daily Values are based on a 2000 calorie diet.

Scandinavian Red Cabbage Soup

(Serves 2)

Ingredients

- 2 cups (475 ml) liquid of choice (stock, broth or bouillon)
- 3/4 cup (50 g) red cabbage (shredded finely)
- 1/4 cup (35 g) sweet potato (washed, peeled and chopped into small pieces)
- 1/2 cup (45 g) yellow onion (peeled and chopped into small pieces)
- 3 cloves garlic (peeled, crushed and minced)
- 1 tbsp olive oil
- Sea salt and pepper to taste (freshly ground)
- 2 tsp caraway seeds
- 2 boiled eggs (halved)

Instructions

1. Heat the olive oil in a pan over low heat. Sauté the onion until fragrant and the onion is translucent.
2. Add the remaining broth, cabbage, caraway seeds and sweet potato.
3. Stir and bring the mixture to a gentle boil.
4. Lower the heat and simmer till the sweet potato and cabbage are tender.
5. Turn off the heat and allow the contents of the pan to cool down thoroughly.

Using the Nutribullet RX:

a) Pour the contents of the pan into your assembled Nutribullet RX cup and blade and blend on soup mode.

b) Season with freshly ground sea salt and pepper.

c) Pour the soup into a serving bowl and serve with the boiled eggs.

Using other Nutribullet models (you may need to blend in two batches):

a) Pour the soup into the Nutribullet cup; blend the soup to your desired texture.

b) Transfer the blended soup back to the pan and heat gently till steaming hot.

c) Season with freshly ground sea salt and pepper.

d) Dish out the soup into a serving bowl and serve with the boiled eggs.

e) Enjoy my version of a Scandinavian soup, fresh and warm.

Nutritional Information

- Calories - 230
- Carbohydrates - 11g - (4%)
- Protein - 12g - (24%)
- Total Fat - 16g - (25%)
- Cholesterol - 186mg - (62%)
- Fibre - 2g - (8%)

Percent Daily Values are based on a 2000 calorie diet.

Cold Summer Berry Soup

(Serves 2)

Ingredients

- 1 cup (240 ml) plain yoghurt
- 1/2 cups (120 ml) dry white wine
- 1/2 cup (120 ml) organic cranberry raspberry juice
- 1/4 cup (30 g) fresh organic raspberries
- 1/4 cup (40 g) organic strawberries (chopped into quarters)
- 1 tbsp coconut sugar or palm syrup
- 1/4 tsp ground cinnamon
- 1/2 cup (70 g) fresh organic blueberries

Instructions for all Nutribullet models:

1. Place all the ingredients in the assembled Nutribullet RX cup and blade or the Nutribullet cup, except for the blueberries, and blend for 5-7 minutes.

2. Transfer to a bowl, stir in the yoghurt, cover and chill for 3 hours.

3. Dish out into a serving bowl, scatter the top with the blueberries and serve immediately.

4. This soup will taste best when chilled.

Nutritional Information

- Calories - 216
- Carbohydrates - 32g - (11%)
- Protein - 7g - (14%)
- Total Fat - 2g - (3%)
- Cholesterol - 8mg - (3%)
- Fibre - 2g - (8%)

Percent Daily Values are based on a 2000 calorie diet.

Brussels Sprouts and Eggplant Soup

(Serves 2)

Ingredients

- 2 cups (475 ml) liquid of choice (stock, broth or bouillon)
- 1/2 cup (45 g) Brussels sprouts (chopped into small pieces)
- 1/2 cup (40 g) eggplant (chopped into small pieces)
- 1/4 cup (40 g) red onion (peeled and chopped into small pieces)
- 1/4 cup (40 g) potato (peeled and chopped into small pieces)
- 2 cloves garlic (peeled, crushed and minced)
- 2 tbsp butter
- Sea salt and pepper to taste (freshly ground)
- 1 cup (240 ml) plain yoghurt
- A handful fresh parsley

Instructions

1. Rub a little salt over the eggplant to prevent oxidization; rinse off the salt before cooking.
2. Heat the butter in a pan over medium heat; sauté the onion and garlic with a splash of broth until fragrant and the onion is translucent.
3. Add the remaining broth, Brussels sprouts, eggplant and sweet potato and bring the mixture to a gentle boil.
4. Lower the heat and simmer till the vegetables are tender.
5. Turn off the heat and allow the contents of the pan to cool down thoroughly.

Using the Nutribullet RX:

a) Pour the contents of the pan into your assembled Nutribullet RX cup and blade and blend on soup mode.

b) Season with freshly ground sea salt and pepper.

c) Pour the soup into a serving bowl, drizzle the yoghurt over the soup. Garnish with parsley and serve.

Using other Nutribullet models (you may need to blend in two batches):

a) Pour the soup into the Nutribullet cup; blend the soup to your desired texture.

b) Transfer the blended soup back to the pan and heat gently till steaming hot.

c) Season with freshly ground sea salt and pepper.

d) Dish out the soup into a serving bowl. Drizzle the yoghurt over the soup.

e) Garnish with parsley and serve.

Nutritional Information

- Calories - 268
- Carbohydrates - 20g - (7%)
- Protein - 13g - (26%)
- Total Fat - 15g - (23%)
- Cholesterol - 39mg - (13%)
- Fibre - 3g - (12%)

Percent Daily Values are based on a 2000 calorie diet.

Chapter 10: Soup Recipes with Superfoods

Black Garlic and Black Bean Soup

(Serves 2)

Ingredients

- 2 cups (475 ml) liquid of choice (stock, broth or bouillon)
- 1/4 cup (35 g) dried black beans
- 1/2 cup (65 g) cucumber (chopped into small pieces)
- 1/2 cup (35 g) kale (chopped finely)
- 1/4 cup (35 g) sweet potato (peeled and chopped into small pieces)
- 1 black garlic bulb (peeled and minced)
- 1 tbsp olive oil
- 1 cup (120 g) pumpkin seeds (shelled and lightly roasted)
- Sea salt and pepper to taste (freshly ground)
- Pinch of chilli powder

Instructions

1. Soak the black beans overnight. Cook the beans in fresh water the next day. Boil till the beans are tender. Drain and set aside.

2. Heat the olive oil in a pan over low heat. Sauté the onion and garlic with a splash of broth and sauté till fragrant and the onion is translucent.

3. Add the remaining broth, sweet potato, chilli powder and beans and bring to a gentle boil.

4. Reduce the heat and simmer until the sweet potato is tender.

5. Stir in the kale and leave the heat on for 1-2 minutes and then turn off the heat.

6. Allow the contents of the pan to cool down thoroughly.

Using the Nutribullet RX:

a) Transfer the contents into your assembled Nutribullet RX cup and blade.

b) Add the cucumber, half the pumpkin seeds and blend on soup mode.

c) Season with freshly ground sea salt and pepper.

d) Pour into a serving bowl; sprinkle the roasted pumpkin seeds over the soup and serve.

Using other Nutribullet models (you may need to blend in two batches):

a) Pour the soup into the Nutribullet cup; blend the soup to your desired texture.

b) Transfer the blended soup back to the pan and heat gently till steaming hot.

c) Season with freshly ground sea salt and pepper.

d) Dish out the soup into a serving bowl.

e) Sprinkle the roasted pumpkin seeds over the soup and serve.

Nutritional Information

- Calories - 575
- Carbohydrates - 25g - (8%)
- Protein - 30g - (60%)
- Total Fat - 40g - (62%)
- Cholesterol - 0.01mg - (0%)
- Fibre - 5g - (20%)

Percent Daily Values are based on a 2000 calorie diet.

Black Bean Soup with Kukicha Broth

(Serves 2)

Ingredients

- 1 tbsp kukicha twigs
- 1/4 cup (35 g) dried black beans
- 1 black garlic bulb (minced)
- 1 cup (160 g) onion (peeled and chopped into small pieces)
- 1/4 tsp dried oregano
- 1/4 tsp paprika
- 1/4 tsp cumin
- 1 jalapeno pepper (seeded and chopped finely)
- 1 tbsp tomato paste
- 1 tbsp olive oil
- Sea salt and pepper to taste (freshly ground)

Instructions

1. Make the kukicha broth by boiling 1 1/2 cups (350 ml) of water, add 1 tbsp of organic kukicha twigs and simmer on low heat for 10 minutes to release the phytonutrients. Turn off the heat and set aside.

2. Soak the black beans overnight and boil in fresh water the next day. Cook till the beans are tender, drain and set aside.

3. Heat the olive oil in a pan over low heat. Sauté the onion till fragrant and the onion is translucent.

4. Add the broth, minced garlic, black beans, jalapeno pepper, paprika, cumin, and oregano and bring to a gentle boil.

5. Turn the heat down and simmer for 10 minutes.

6. Turn off the heat and allow the contents of the pan to cool thoroughly.

Using the Nutribullet RX:

a) Transfer the soup in your assembled Nutribullet RX cup and blade.

b) Add the tomato paste and blend on soup mode.

c) Season with freshly ground sea salt and pepper and serve.

Using other Nutribullet models (you may need to blend in two batches):

a) Pour the soup into the Nutribullet cup, add the tomato paste and blend the soup to your desired texture.

b) Transfer the blended soup back to the pan and heat gently till steaming hot.

c) Season with freshly ground sea salt and pepper.

d) Dish out the soup into a serving bowl and serve.

Nutritional Information

- Calories - 176
- Carbohydrates - 26g - (9%)
- Protein - 5g - (10%)
- Total Fat - 7g - (11%)
- Fibre - 4g - (16%)

Percent Daily Values are based on a 2000 calorie diet.

Jerusalem Artichoke and Chickpea Soup

(Serves 2)

Ingredients

- 1 cup (240 ml) liquid of choice (stock, broth or bouillon)
- 1 cup (240 ml) coconut milk
- 1 cup (150 g) Jerusalem artichoke (peeled and chopped into small pieces)
- 1/4 cup (40 g) dried chickpeas
- 1 cup (100 g) shallots (peeled and chopped)
- 2 cloves garlic (peeled, crushed and minced)
- 2 tsp ground fresh ginger
- 1/4 tsp turmeric powder
- 1/4 tsp cumin powder
- 1/2 tbsp curry powder
- 1/2 tbsp ghee
- Sea salt and pepper to taste (freshly ground)

Instructions

1. Soak the chickpeas in water overnight. Boil the beans in fresh water till tender. Drain and set aside.

2. Heat the ghee in a pan over medium to high heat. Sauté the shallots, garlic, ginger, turmeric, cumin and curry powder with a splash of broth till fragrant.

3. Add in the remaining broth, coconut milk, artichoke, cooked chickpeas, black garlic and thyme and bring to a gentle boil.

4. Lower the heat and simmer till the artichoke is tender.

5. Turn off the heat and allow the contents of the pan to cool thoroughly.

Using the Nutribullet RX:

a) Transfer to your assembled Nutribullet RX cup and blade and blend on soup mode.

b) Season with freshly ground sea salt and pepper.

c) Pour into a serving bowl and serve piping hot.

Using other Nutribullet models (you may need to blend in two batches):

a) Pour the soup into the Nutribullet cup and blend the soup to your desired texture.

b) Transfer the blended soup back to the pan and heat gently till steaming hot.

c) Season with freshly ground sea salt and pepper.

d) Dish out the soup into a serving bowl and serve hot.

Nutritional Information

- Calories - 413
- Carbohydrates - 36g - (12%)
- Protein - 8g - (16%)
- Total Fat - 29g - (45%)
- Cholesterol - 9mg - (3%)
- Fibre - 4g - (16%)

Percent Daily Values are based on a 2000 calorie diet.

Fennel and Beet Soup

(Serves 2)

Ingredients

- 1 cup (240 ml) liquid of choice (stock, broth or bouillon)
- 1 cup (240 ml) plain yoghurt
- 3/4 cup (100 g) beet (peeled and chopped into small pieces)
- 3/4 cup (65 g) fennel bulb (chopped into small pieces)
- 1/4 cup (40 g) onion (peeled and chopped into small pieces)
- 2 cloves garlic (peeled, crushed and minced)
- 1 tbsp olive oil
- 1/2 tsp fennel seeds
- Sea salt (freshly ground) to taste
- 1/2 cup (5 g) fennel fronds (chopped)

Instructions

1. Heat the oil in a pan over low heat. Stir in the onion, garlic, fennel seeds and chopped fennel with a splash of broth and sauté until the fennel is tender.
2. Add the remaining broth and beet and bring to a gentle boil.
3. Lower the heat and simmer until the beet is tender.
4. Turn off the heat and allow thorough cooling of the contents.
5. The blending will have to be done in two batches.

Using the Nutribullet RX:

a) Add the contents to your assembled Nutribullet RX cup and blade and blend on soup mode.

b) Season with freshly ground sea salt and pepper.

c) Pour out into a serving bowl; whisk in the plain yoghurt.

d) Garnish with the fennel fronds and serve.

Using other Nutribullet models (you may need to blend in two batches):

a) Pour the soup into the Nutribullet cup and blend the soup to your desired texture.

b) Transfer the blended soup back to the pan and heat gently till steaming hot.

c) Season with freshly ground sea salt and pepper; whisk in the plain yoghurt.

d) Dish out the soup into a serving bowl and garnish with the fennel fronds and serve.

Nutritional Information

- Calories - 203
- Carbohydrates - 20g - (7%)
- Protein - 11g - (22%)
- Total Fat - 10g - (15%)
- Cholesterol - 8mg - (3%)
- Fibre - 3g - (12%)

Percent Daily Values are based on a 2000 calorie diet.

Creamy Avocado Soup

(Serves 2)

Ingredients

- 1 cup (240 ml) water
- 1 cup (240 ml) plain yoghurt
- 1/2 cup (75 g) avocado (peeled, stoned and chopped)
- 1/2 cup (55 g) cashew nuts (chopped into small pieces)
- 1/4 cup (4 g) fresh cilantro/coriander (finely chopped)
- 1/2 cup (80 g) onion (peeled and chopped into small pieces)
- 1/2 tbsp balsamic vinegar
- 2 tsp premium green tea powder (matcha)
- Sea salt and white pepper (freshly ground) to taste
- A handful fresh chives (finely chopped)

Instructions for all Nutribullet models:

1. Whisk the matcha in 1/4 cup of water and ensure there are no lumps.
2. Add in the remaining water and mix thoroughly.
3. Add all the ingredients to your Nutribullet cup and blend for 7-10 minutes.
4. Garnish with fresh chives and serve immediately.
5. The blending may need to be done in two batches.

Nutritional Information

- Calories - 322
- Carbohydrates - 27g - (9%)
- Protein - 14g - (28%)
- Total Fat - 20g - (31%)
- Cholesterol - 8mg - (3%)
- Fibre - 5g - (20%)

Percent Daily Values are based on a 2000 calorie diet.

Pear and Green Tea Soup

(Serves 2)

Ingredients

- 1 1/2 cups (350 ml) water
- 1/2 cup (120 ml) plain yoghurt
- 1/2 cup (35 g) kale (chopped)
- 1/4 cup (40 g) pears (chopped into small pieces)
- 1/2 cup (75 g) ripe avocado (peeled, pitted and chopped)
- 1/2 tsp ground clove
- 1 vanilla bean
- 1 tbsp honey
- 1 orange (juice and zest)
- 2 tbsp chia seeds
- Sea salt (freshly ground) to taste
- 2 tsp green tea powder (premium grade matcha)
- A handful fresh mint leaves

Instructions

Preparing the matcha:

1. Whisk the matcha in 1/4 cup (60 ml) of water to ensure the matcha powder is well mixed and there are no lumps.
2. Add in the remaining water and mix thoroughly. Set aside the matcha tea.

Preparing the kale:

1. Steam the kale for 3-4 minutes, until kale leaves turn bright green.
2. Rinse the steamed kale and set aside.

Using the Nutribullet RX:

a) Add all the ingredients to your assembled Nutribullet RX cup and blade.

b) Blend for 5-7 minutes for a smooth consistency.

c) Transfer soup into a serving bowl and serve immediately, garnished with fresh mint leaves.

Using other Nutribullet models (you may need to blend in two batches):

a) Add the ingredients to your Nutribullet cup and blend for 5-7 minutes for a smooth consistency.

b) Transfer soup into a serving bowl and serve immediately, garnished with fresh mint leaves.

Nutritional Information

- Calories - 265
- Carbohydrates - 36g - (12%)
- Protein - 8g - (16%)
- Total Fat - 12g - (18%)
- Cholesterol - 4mg - (1%)
- Fibre - 12g - (48%)

Percent Daily Values are based on a 2000 calorie diet.

Mushroom and Winter Chestnut Soup

(Serves 2)

Ingredients

- 3 tsp of loose pau d'arco
- 1 cup (240 ml) water
- 1/2 cup (35 g) mushrooms (finely chopped)
- 1/2 cup (65 g) jicama (peeled and chopped)
- 1/4 cup (35 g) chestnuts (cooked, shelled and finely chopped)
- 1/4 cup (40 g) onion (peeled and chopped into small pieces)
- 2 cloves garlic (peeled, crushed and minced)
- 1 tbsp avocado oil
- 1 tsp ground nutmeg
- Sea salt and pepper to taste (freshly ground)

Instructions

Method for making pau d'arco tea:

1. Add 3 tsp of loose pau d'arco to 2 cups (475 ml) of boiling water and simmer over low heat for 5-7 minutes. This will release the phytonutrients.

Method:

1. Cut slits in chestnuts. Roast the chestnuts in the oven, 300 °F (150°C, Gas 2) for about 20 minutes. Remove from the oven and remove the shell while the chestnuts are warm. Chop the chestnuts and set aside.

2. Heat the oil in a large pan over medium heat; sauté the onion and garlic with a splash of water and cook until fragrant and the onion is translucent.

3. Add the pau d'arco tea, jicama, chestnuts, mushrooms and nutmeg to the pan and bring it to a gentle boil.

4. Turn down the heat and simmer for 10 minutes.

5. Turn off the heat and allow the contents of the pan to cool thoroughly.

Using the Nutribullet RX:

a) Add the contents to your assembled Nutribullet RX cup and blade and blend on soup mode.

b) Season with freshly ground sea salt and pepper.

c) Pour out into a serving bowl and serve.

Using other Nutribullet models (you may need to blend in two batches):

a) Pour the soup into the Nutribullet cup and blend the soup to your desired texture.

b) Transfer the blended soup back to the pan and heat gently till steaming hot.

c) Season with freshly ground sea salt and pepper.

d) Dish out the soup into a serving bowl and serve.

Recipe Notes

Not all brands of pau d'arco bark taste the same; some taste better than others. Using loose pau d'arco bark will produce stronger tasting tea.

Nutritional Information

- Calories - 158
- Carbohydrates - 19g - (6%)
- Protein - 3g - (6%)
- Total Fat - 8g - (12%)
- Fibre - 5g - (20%)

Percent Daily Values are based on a 2000 calorie diet.

Sweet Creamy Adzuki Beans and Date Soup

(Serves 2)

Ingredients

- 1 cup (240 ml) coconut milk
- 1 cup (240 ml) water
- 1 1/2 tsp of loose pau d'arco
- 2 tbsp dried adzuki beans
- 1/4 cup (45 g) dates (stoned and chopped into small pieces)
- 2 tsp honey

Instructions

1. Add 1 1/2 tsp of loose pau d'arco bark to a cup of boiling water and simmer over low heat for 10 minutes to release the phytonutrients. Turn off the heat and set aside.

2. Soak the adzuki beans overnight. Discard the water the next day and boil in fresh water and cook till the beans are tender. Drain and set aside.

3. Pour the pau d'arco tea into a pan, add in the beans and dates and bring to a gentle boil.

4. Turn the heat down and simmer for 10-15 minutes.

5. Turn off the heat and cool thoroughly.

Using the Nutribullet RX:

a) Transfer the contents into your assembled Nutribullet RX blade and cup.

b) Add the honey and coconut milk and blend.

c) Pour into a serving bowl and serve.

d) If you prefer, chill for 1-2 hours and serve cold.

Using other models of Nutribullet (you may need to blend in two batches):

a) Transfer the contents into your Nutribullet cup; add the honey and coconut milk and blend on soup mode.

b) Pour into a serving bowl and serve.

c) If you prefer, chill for 1-2 hours and serve cold.

Nutritional Information

- Calories - 330
- Carbohydrates - 35g - (12%)
- Protein - 4g - (8%)
- Total Fat - 22g - (34%)
- Fibre - 4g - (16%)

Percent Daily Values are based on a 2000 calorie diet.

Kale with Black Bean Soup

(Serves 2)

Ingredients

- 1 1/2 tbsp of organic kukicha twigs
- 1/4 cup (35 g) dried black beans
- 1/2 cup (35 g) kale (chopped)
- 1/4 cup (40 g) onion (peeled and chopped into small pieces)
- 2 cloves garlic (peeled, crushed and minced)
- 1/2 tsp dried oregano
- 1/2 tsp dried basil
- 1 jalapeno pepper (seeded and chopped)
- 1 tbsp tomato paste
- 1 tbsp olive oil
- Sea salt and pepper to taste (freshly ground)
- A handful fresh basil (chopped)

Instructions

1. Make the kukicha broth by boiling 2 cups (475 ml) of water, add 1 1/2 tbsp of organic kukicha twigs and simmer on low heat for 10 minutes to release the phytonutrients. Set aside.

2. Soak the black beans overnight, boil in fresh water the next day and cook till tender. Drain and set aside.

3. Heat the olive oil in a pan over low heat. Sauté the onion, garlic, oregano, basil and tomato paste with a splash of water till fragrant and the onion is translucent.

4. Add the kukicha tea, cooked black beans and jalapeno pepper and bring to a gentle boil.

5. Turn the heat down and simmer for 5-7 minutes. Stir in the kale and leave on the heat for 1-2 minutes.

6. Turn off the heat and allow the contents of the pan to cool thoroughly.

Using the Nutribullet RX:

a) Transfer the soup into your assembled Nutribullet RX cup and blade and blend on soup mode.

b) Season with freshly ground sea salt and pepper.

c) Pour in a serving bowl, garnish with the basil and serve.

Using other Nutribullet models (you may need to blend in two batches):

a) Pour the soup into the Nutribullet cup and blend the soup to your desired texture.

b) Transfer the blended soup back to the pan and heat gently till steaming hot.

c) Season with freshly ground sea salt and pepper.

d) Dish out the soup into a serving bowl, garnish with the basil and serve.

Nutritional Information

- Calories - 145
- Carbohydrates - 19g - (6%)
- Protein - 5g - (10%)
- Total Fat - 7g - (11%)
- Fibre - 4g - (16%)

Percent Daily Values are based on a 2000 calorie diet.

Creamy Nutrient-Dense Vegetable Soup

(Serves 2)

Ingredients

- 1 cup (240 ml) liquid of choice (stock, broth or bouillon)
- 1 cup (240 ml) coconut milk
- 1/4 cup (25 g) cauliflower (chopped into small pieces)
- 1/2 cup (15 g) organic spinach (chopped)
- 1 cup (35 g) watercress (washed)
- 1/4 cup (40 g) onion (peeled and chopped into small pieces)
- 2 cloves garlic (peeled, crushed and minced)
- 1 tbsp butter
- 2 tsp green tea powder (cooking grade matcha)
- Sea salt and pepper to taste (freshly ground)

Instructions

1. Heat the butter in a pan over low to medium heat. Sauté the onion and garlic, with a splash of water till fragrant and the onion is translucent.
2. Add the water and cauliflower and bring to a gentle boil.
3. Turn the heat down and simmer till the cauliflower is cooked.
4. Add in the spinach and watercress and turn the heat off after 2 minutes.
5. Allow the contents of the pan to cool.
6. Whisk the matcha powder in the coconut milk.

Using the Nutribullet RX:

a) Transfer the cooled contents in the pan into your assembled Nutribullet RX cup and blade. The blending will have to be done in two stages.
b) Add in the coconut milk and matcha mix and blend on soup mode.

c) Season with freshly ground sea salt and pepper.

d) Pour in a serving bowl and serve.

Using other Nutribullet models (you may need to blend in two batches):

a) Pour the soup into the Nutribullet cup.

b) Add in the coconut milk and matcha mix and blend the soup to your desired texture. The blending will have to be done in two stages.

c) Transfer the blended soup back to the pan and heat gently till steaming hot.

d) Season with freshly ground sea salt and pepper.

e) Dish out the soup into a serving bowl and serve.

Nutritional Information

- Calories - 298
- Carbohydrates - 10g - (3%)
- Protein - 5g - (10%)
- Total Fat - 28g - (43%)
- Cholesterol - 16mg - (5%)
- Fibre - 2g - (8%)

Percent Daily Values are based on a 2000 calorie diet.

I Hope You Have Enjoyed Reading My Book

Please consider leaving an honest review

Reviews are important for readers when considering reading a book. Your views are important. Please leave an honest review.

Review link that re-directs to your regional Amazon:

myBook.to/ShawSoup

Made in the USA
Las Vegas, NV
24 February 2024

86148778R00090